STUDY GUIDE
for

The Enjoyment of Music

Tenth Edition

STUDY GUIDE
for

The Enjoyment of Music

TENTH EDITION

Kristine Forney

CALIFORNIA STATE UNIVERSITY, LONG BEACH

 W • W • NORTON & COMPANY • NEW YORK • LONDON

ISBN 10: 0-393-92891-8 (pbk.)
ISBN 13: 978-0-393-92891-4 (pbk.)

W. W. Norton & Company, Inc., 500 Fifth Avenue, New York, N.Y. 10110
    www.wwnorton.com
W. W. Norton & Company Ltd., Castle House, 75/76 Wells Street, London W1T 3QT

1 2 3 4 5 6 7 8 9 0

Contents

Preface

This Study Guide, which accompanies *The Enjoyment of Music,* Tenth Edition, is designed to help you get the most out of your music studies by reinforcing the information in the text and by guiding you in the exploration of new musical styles. This workbook is organized to coincide with the Regular and Shorter versions of the text. Exercises throughout the guide are keyed to chapters, Listening Guides (LG), and Cultural Perspectives (CP) in both versions of the book. In this Guide you will find the following:

- Forty-three *Review* exercises, based on the most important terms, concepts, and historical information in the text. These exercises test your knowledge and understanding through objective questions (multiple choice, true/false, matching, and short answer). For some questions, you are asked to consider an idea and give your opinion. These questions are designed to help you prepare for exams and quizzes. Your instructor may assign review exercises to be completed and turned in (you will notice that the pages are perforated for easy removal) or may suggest that you do them on your own to reinforce your studying.

- Forty-three *Listen* exercises that help guide your study of the musical selections outlined in the text (in Listening Guides) and included on the recording set. Note that each question about works that are included *only* on the larger 8-CD set of *The Norton Recordings* (which accompanies the Regular version of the text) has an asterisk (*) next to it; if you are using the Shorter text and the 4-CD set, you should skip the asterisked items. The *Listen* questions ask you to describe certain musical elements you hear and also to review the history and form of each work. Before completing each listening exercise, you should read about the work and listen to it while following the Listening Guide in the text or the electronic Listening Guides (eLGs) on your Student Resource Disc.

- Twenty-three *Explore* studies that review your understanding of the information presented in the Cultural Perspectives throughout the text. These guides are designed to broaden your knowledge of traditional, popular, and certain non-Western musics and how they have influenced Western art music or been influenced by it. Some Cultural Perspectives place music and musicians in context within related disciplines, to help you integrate knowledge from your other studies. For each of these exercises, there is an outside assignment suggested (listening from iMusic or Web-based) that encourages you to explore another style of music and write about it. The Cultural Perspectives online (at StudySpace) have links to enhanced learning materials. These exercises may be assigned by the instructor as either required or extra-credit work, or you may decide which exercises you are most interested in doing outside of class.

- Fifteen *Music Activities* that allow you more direct and sometimes "hands-on" experience with music. These may be assigned to you as solo activities, as Web-based, or for use in study groups or discussion sections. The introduction to this section on page 219 provides more information about these guides.

- Five *Concert Report* outlines for completion during or after concerts. Since most music appreciation classes require concert attendance and written reports, these forms may be completed and turned in or may serve as outlines for prose reports, depending on course requirements. The introduction to this section on page 251 lists the different outlines provided and the types of music for which each should be used. Included are a sample completed outline based on a hypothetical concert and a sample prose report.

Note too that you can use the *Enjoyment of Music* StudySpace as an alternate (or additional) means of reviewing terms and listening, and exploring the Cultural Perspectives from the text. You may access this site at www.wwnorton.com/enjoy.

This Study Guide also includes two surveys: one to complete at the beginning of the course and one to fill out at its close. Instructors may wish to collect these surveys to familiarize themselves with the musical tastes and experiences of their students, or you may use them to gauge how your own tastes and experiences have changed as a result of taking the class, reading *The Enjoyment of Music* text, and using the accompanying materials.

I wish to express my sincere appreciation to the many faculty who have offered helpful suggestions for this edition of the guide, to my colleagues at California State University, Long Beach, for their contributions and unflagging loyalty, and to the many students on whom I have tried out these exercises. Through the use of these materials, they arrived, as I hope you will, at a new "enjoyment of music." I am much indebted to Maribeth Payne, music editor at W. W. Norton, Kathryn Talalay, our very capable project manager for this new edition of *The Enjoyment of Music*, and Courtney Fitch for her adept copyediting of this study guide.

Kristine Forney

Note on Abbreviations

Throughout this Study Guide, the following abbreviations are used:

Sh   = Shorter version of the text
LG   = Listening Guide
CP   = Cultural Perspective
*e***LG**   = Electronic Listening Guide (software on Student Res urce Disc)
iMusic = iMusic on Student Resource Disc

References to the two versions of the book are given by chapter num ber; use the Table of Contents in your textbook to locate the page number for each chapter. References to Listening Guides are given by LG num ers and to Cultural Perspectives by CP numbers. For quick access to these ages in the text, consult the Tables of Cultural Perspectives and Listening Guides in the front of your textbook. A Table of Listening Guides and Reco dings is printed inside the covers of your textbook to help you locate the musical selections on whichever recordings package you are using.

NAME Vickie Flores   DATE 1/28/08 CLASS _____

Pre-Course Survey

Level: ___ Freshman X Sophomore ___ Junior ___ Senior ___ Grad

___ High school ___ Adult education Other _____

General Information

Major (or undeclared): ___English_____

Minor (or undeclared): ___Communications_____

Why did you choose to take this course?

    X general education credit ___ free elective   ___ enjoy music

    ___ required for major   ___ convenient time   ___ instructor

How did you hear about this course?

    X recommended by adviser ___ recommended by student(s)

    ___ found on my own   ___ other _____

Musical Tastes

How often do you listen to music? X frequently   ___ sometimes

                                    ___ infrequently   ___ never

What music listening equipment do you have available?

    X radio X cassette X CD player X CD-ROM drive

    X iPod/MP3 player X car stereo other _____

What styles of music do you prefer to listen to? R & B _____

_____

Name two favorite compositions (in any style).

"I hate that I love you"- Rihanna (R & B)

"Mujer que Camina"- Alejandro Filio (Classical/Latin)

List two favorite performers or performing groups.

Frank Sinatra

Frankie J

Do you attend live concerts? ___ often ___ occasionally X rarely ___ never

If yes, name one you particularly enjoyed.

Tyrone Wells

Musical Background

Check the musical experiences that apply.

_X_ Played an instrument   Which instrument? _guitar_

_X_ Took music lessons   How many years? _5_

_X_ Played or sang in a group

    _X_ concert band   ___ orchestra   ___ chorus   ___ rock band

    ___ musical theater   ___ jazz ensemble   _X_ church choir

    other _____

___ Studied music theory or music appreciation

Which of the following types of concerts have you attended? Name the group or a work performed, if you remember.

___ orchestra _____

___ opera _____

___ musical _____

___ ballet _____

___ concert band _____

___ jazz band _____

___ rock band _____

___ choir/chorus _____

_X_ solo recital _Bethany music recitals_

___ chamber group _____

___ world music _____

___ folk music _____

_X_ other _private performance_

What do you hope to learn in this course? _Why this class is important_

_____

_____

_____

---

1. *Explore* **Music and Sound**
CP 1

Exercises

1. Describe what differentiates a sound or noise from a musical sound.
   A musical sound has a perceivable pitch and a measurable frequency which depends on the vibrating object; whereas a sound or noise has unperceivable pitch and frequency.

2. What are two terms that refer to the loudness or softness of a sound? What measurement unit describes this aspect of a sound?
   Pitch (highness and lowness of a sound) and frequency (# of vibrations/second). The measurement unit describing this aspect of sound is Hertz.

3. Which is the technical term for pitch? ___C___
   a. texture   b. amplitude   c. frequency   d. timbre

   Which is the unit of measurement for pitch? ___a___
   a. hertz   b. watts   c. decibels   d. hexad

4. How did the ancient Greeks and Romans view music in their lives?
   The Greeks and Romans viewed music not only as the force that unified the human body and soul but also as an all-pervading force in the universe, whose arithmetical ratios kept the planets in their orbits.

5. Blowing through a short tube produces a __higher__ (higher or lower) pitch than blowing through a long tube.

6. How do the universe and its bodies produce sound? How can we measure these sounds?
   The sounds (vibrations) produced by black holes in the universe and by the earth—both emit tones that are inaudible to the human ear but can be measured with scientific equipment (i.e.: seismographs)

7. The general music symbol that is used to notate pitch is called a __note__.

8. What is another term for non-amplified music? __acoustic music__

Essay

Write an essay describing the acoustic characteristics that are desirable in a concert hall. Describe an acoustic experience you have had listening to live music (of any style) and comment on the venue (performance site) where you experienced this event.

Or visit StudySpace (www.wwnorton.com/enjoy), read this Cultural Perspective, and follow links provided there. Write an essay describing your online research.

According to the text and online, references — non-amplified or acoustic music require exact and precise engineering for optimum sound reflection. Basically meaning, that the quality of music will be affected by its surrounding environment. I learned four important elements (terms) reguarding the quality of acoustic music and where it is performed: reverberation, reflections, noise reduction coefficient, and sound transmission class. Reverberation are the multiple sound reflections or the time it takes for a sound to no longer be audible; reverberation varies with the amount of space sound has to travel. Reflections or the reflected sound off of a space or surface influence the quality of sound as well. Reflection of sound are controlled by the shape and material a space is made out of (ie. round, wooden playing hall). The noise reduction coefficient is how the material in a space absorbs sound; in other words this is the sound-absorbing capability of the materials used to build the space (including and influenced by: ceiling, floor, and furniture). Sound transmission class has to do with the isolation of a sound depending on all and any penetration, air-gaps, or flanking paths (vents and such) that will degrade the quality of sound.

---

2. *Review* **Elements of Music: Melody and Rhythm**
Chaps. 1–2

Terms to Remember

melody ✓	countermelody ✓	simple meter
interval ✓	rhythm	duple ✓
range ✓	meter	triple ✓
contour ✓	measure	quadruple ✓
type of movement	measure (bar) line	compound meter
conjunct ✓	beat	sextuple meter ✓
disjunct ✓	unaccented ✓	additive meter
structure of melody	accented ✓	downbeat
phrase ✓	nonmetric	upbeat
cadence ✓		syncopation ✓
climax		polyrhythm

Exercises

Complete the following questions.

1. The distance between two different pitches is a(n) _interval_.

2. A(n) _melody_ is a coherent succession of pitches, heard as a unity.

3. A melody that moves by small intervals in a connected style is _conjunct_, while one with many leaps is _disjunct_.

4. The characteristic of a melody that describes its movement up and down is _contour_, and the distance between its highest and lowest notes defines its _range_.

5. A resting point in a melody is known as a(n) _cadence_.

6. The melody of *Amazing Grace* (on p. 14 of the text) is organized into four equal parts known as _(musical) phrases_.

7. A melody heard against the principal tune is called a(n) _countermelody_.

8. The regular pulse and basic unit of length heard in most Western music is called the _beat_.

9. Those pulses that are stronger than others are known as _accent_ _primary/accented_, while weaker pulses are called _Secondary accent_ _/unaccented_.

10. The organizing factor in music that sets fixed time patterns is called _meters_.

3

11. Meters that subdivide beats into groups of two are called _duple meter_.

12. Meters that subdivide beats into groups of three are called _triple meter_.

13. The meter of the folk song *Greensleeves* is best described as _sextuple meter_. Rather than beginning on the downbeat (the first beat of the measure), it starts on a(n) _upbeat_.

14. The most likely meter for a march would be _duple_.

15. The rhythmic procedure that is used to temporarily upset or throw off the meter is called _syncopation_.

16. The simultaneous use of two or more rhythmic patterns is called _polyrhythm_, and is heard in _jazz and rock_ styles.

17. Groupings of irregular numbers of beats that add up to a larger overall pattern produce a(n) _additive_ meter.

18. Music with a veiled beat or no perceptible pulse may be considered _nonmetric_.

iMusic Listening (Student Resource Disc)

Foster: *Camptown Races* (answer questions 19–21 below)

19. Is the opening of the melody principally:
___ conjunct (connected, smooth) or _✓_ disjunct (disjointed, with leaps)?

20. Is the overall range of the melody:
_✓_ narrow (spanning few notes) or ___ wide (spanning many notes)?

21. Is the contour of the melody best described as:
_✓_ wavelike or ___ a straight line?

Simple Gifts (answer questions 22–23 below)
Draw measure lines in the example below.

Text:	'Tis	the	gift		to	be	sim-ple,	tis	the	gift		to	be	free,
Meter:	2		1		2		1	2		1		2		1

22. Which meter is indicated in the example? ___ simple _✓_ compound

23. On what beat does the song begin? _offbeat_

El Cihualteco

24. What metric device(s) is/are used in this mariachi tune (check as many as you hear):
_✓_ changing meter _✓_ syncopation ___ regular phrases

Hildegard: Kyrie

25. Which term best describes the meter of this chant?
___ triple ___ polymetric _✓_ nonmetric

4

3. *Review* Elements of Music: Harmony and Texture
Chaps. 3–4

Terms to Remember

harmony ✓	tonic	scale	texture	counterpoint
chord	tonality	major	monophonic ✓	imitation
scale	syllables	minor	heterophonic ✓	canon
octave	dissonance	diatonic	polyphonic ✓	round
triad ✓	consonance	chromatic	homophonic	
		drone ✓	homorhythmic	

Exercises

Complete the following questions.

1. The element of music that pertains to the movement and relationship of intervals and chords is ___harmony___.

2. What are the syllables used to identify the tones of the scale?
   _do_ re mi fa sol la ti do

3. An octave is the interval from *do* to ___do___ in the scale.

4. The interval of a fifth in syllables is *do* to ___sol___.

5. Three or more tones sounded together are called a(n) ___triad___.

6. A triad is a three-note chord built from alternate scale tones, such as _do_ mi sol. In numbers, it would be scale tones 1 3 5.

7. In the organizing system known as tonality, the first scale tone, or keynote, is the ___tonic___.

8. The two scale types commonly found in Western music from around 1650 to 1900 are ___major___ and ___minor___.

9. Music built from the tones of one of the scale types above is referred to as ___diatonic___, while music built from the full range of notes in the octave is referred to as ___chromatic___

10. On which scale would a lament probably be built? ___minor___

11. Unstable musical sounds in need of resolution are called ___dissonance___. How might they sound? ___discordant (tense)___

12. Musical sounds that seem stable, not needing to resolve, are called
consonance. How might they sound? concordant (agreeable)

13. Some musics unfold over a supporting sustained tone, or __drone__.

14. The element of music that refers to its fabric or the interplay of its
parts is known as __texture__.

15. Music with a single melodic line and no accompaniment has a
__monophonic__ texture, whereas music with a single melody and a
chordal accompaniment has a __homophonic__ texture.

16. A texture in which all voices move together with the same rhythm,
note-against-note, is called __polyphonic__.

17. __Heterophonic__ is a texture that combines two or more melodic voices.

18. A melody combined with an ornamented version of itself produces a
texture known as __heterophonic__. In what styles of music does
this frequently occur? __jazz and spirituals__

19. Overlapping statements of the same melody in several parts is known as
__round__, which produces a __polyphonic__ texture.

20. A strictly ordered composition based on one voice imitating another is
called a __imitation__, or, more popularly, a __canon__.

iMusic Listening (Student Resource Disc)

Handel: *Alla hornpipe* from *Water Music* (answer questions 21–23 below)

21. Which term describes the harmony? _✓_ consonant ___ dissonant

22. Do you think this dance is in _✓_ major or ___ minor tonality?

23. Which term describes the texture? _✓_ polyphonic ___ homophonic

Bach: Toccata in D minor

24. Which term best describes the opening texture?
_✓_ monophonic ___ homophonic

Catán: Interlude, from *Rappaccini's Daughter*, chord

25. Would you consider this chord ___ consonant or _✓_ dissonant?

Handel: "Hallelujah Chorus," from *Messiah*

26. What term best describes the texture of the opening text (on the word
"Hallelujah")?
___ polyphonic ___ heterophonic _✓_ homorhythmic

---

4. *Review* **Elements of Music: Form**
Chap. 5

Terms to Remember

form	binary form	strophic form
repetition ✓	ternary form	call and response
contrast ✓	theme	ostinato ✓
variation ✓	motive ✓	movement ✓
improvisation	sequence ✓	

Exercises

Complete the following questions.

1. The element of music representing clarity and order is __form__ .

2. The two basic principles of musical structure are __repitition__ and __contrast__. A third principle of form is __variation__.

3. Binary form can best be outlined as __two-part__. Which principle of form (from question 2) is central to this scheme? __repitition__

4. Ternary form can best be outlined as __three-part__. Which principles of form does this structure illustrate? __contrast__

5. Pieces created by performers during the performance (as opposed to precomposed pieces) are based on __improvisation__ . In which styles of music is this technique common? __jazz, rock, and non-Western style music__

6. A __theme__ is a melody used as a building block in a work. This melody can be broken up into smaller units, also known as __motive__ , or it can be restated at another pitch level, also known as __sequence__.

7. The repetitive singing style in which a leader is imitated by a group of followers is called __call and response__ . In which musical cultures is this style common? __African, Native American, African-American__

8. The structural procedure whereby a short pattern—melodic, rhythmic, or harmonic—is repeated is called __ostinato__ .

9. The sections of a large-scale work are called __movements__ .

iMusic Listening (Student Resource Disc)

Brahms: *Lullaby*

10. Which best describes the form? ✓ strophic ___ binary ___ ternary

Amazing Grace

11. Which formal procedure is heard in this performance?

✓ variation ___ improvisation ___ repetition

Battle Hymn of the Republic

12. Which formal technique is most obvious in this song?

___ repetition ✓ contrast ___ improvisation

Beethoven: *Für Elise*

13. Which of the following formal procedures is more used in this work?

✓ repetition ___ contrast

Purcell: Rondeau, from *Suite de symphonies*

14. In this dance, a repetition pattern occurs after the first melodic phrase whereby an idea is stated four times, each time starting on a different pitch. This technique is considered: ___ variation ✓ sequence

Beethoven: Symphony No. 5, I

15. This familiar orchestral work opens with a: ___ theme ___ motive

Osain

16. What formal procedure is heard in this selection?

___ ostinato ✓ call and response

Minuet in D minor (*Anna Magdalena Notebook*)

17. Which form best describes this dance?

✓ binary ___ ternary ___ strophic

18. Consider how binary and ternary form might occur in nature or in the visual arts. Cite an example of each form.

_____

_____

_____

_____

---

5. *Review* **Elements of Music: Tempo and Dynamics**
Chap. 6

Terms to Remember

tempo	tempo (continued)	dynamics
accelerando	*moderato*	*crescendo*
adàgio	*molto*	*decrescendo*
allegro	*non troppo*	*diminuendo*
andante	*poco*	*forte*
a tempo	*presto*	*fortissimo*
grave	*ritardando*	*mezzo piano*
largo	*vivace*	*mezzo forte*
meno		*piano*
		pianissimo
		sforzando

Exercises

Complete the following questions.

1. The standard Italian term for a fast, cheerful tempo is ___allegro___ .

2. The Italian modifier meaning "not too much" is ___non troppo___ .

3. What tempo is even faster than the answer to question 1? ___presto___

4. A slow tempo at pace of walking is ___andante___

5. The indication to become gradually slower is ___ritardando___ ;
   to become gradually faster is ___accelerando___ .

6. A return to the original tempo would be indicated as ___tempo___ .

7. A tempo marking of *poco a poco adagio* means ___a little___ .

8. A tempo of *molto vivace* would be best interpreted as ___very lively___ .

9. The dynamic marking for soft is ___piano (p)___ and for loud, ___forte (f)___ .

10. Growing gradually louder is indicated by ___<___ ; growing
    gradually softer is indicated by ___>___ .

11. A sudden stress or accent is called for by a ___sforzando (sf)___ .

True or False

___T___ 12. Dynamics in music can affect our emotional reactions.

___F___ 13. Nineteenth-century musical scores generally lack indications for
    dynamics or tempo.

_F_ 14. A change in volume from *mp* to *f* would be indicated by a *diminuendo*.

_T_ 15. The softest dynamic marking ever used is *pp*.

____ 16. Tempo and dynamics contribute to the overall musical expression of a piece.

iMusic Listening (Student Resource Disc)

Mozart: Clarinet Concerto, II

17. Which tempo marking is most appropriate for this work?

_X_ adagio ___ moderato ___ allegro

Rossini: *William Tell* Overture

18. Which tempo marking is most appropriate for this fanfare?

___ adagio ___ moderato _X_ allegro

19. What device does the composer use in this familiar theme?

___ accelerando _X_ crescendo

Bizet: *Toreador Song* from *Carmen*

20. Which tempo marking is most appropriate for this work?

___ adagio _X_ moderato ___ allegro

Haydn: *Surprise* Symphony

21. Which dynamic marking is most appropriate for the opening?

___ piano _X_ mezzo forte ___ forte

22. Which marking would suit the "surprise" chord near the beginning?

___ pianissimo _X_ fortissimo ___ diminuendo

Wagner: *Ride of the Valkyries*

23. Which tempo marking is most appropriate for this famous selection?

___ adagio _X_ moderato ___ allegro

24. Which dynamic device does the composer use in this passage?

___ accelerando ___ decrescendo _X_ crescendo

Beethoven: *Ode to Joy*

25. Which dynamic marking is most appropriate for this passage?

___ mezzo forte _X_ forte ___ fortissimo

Simple Gifts

26. Which tempo variation technique is heard at the close of this folk song setting? ___ crescendo ___ accelerando _X_ ritardando

6. *Review* World Musical Instruments, Ensembles, and Their Contexts
   Chaps. 7–10

Exercises

Match the following instruments with their category of sound production (use choices as many times as needed).

_c_ 1. gourd rattle   a. aerophone

_b_ 2. ukelele   b. chordophone

_a_ 3. bagpipe   c. idiophone

_b_ 4. Indian sitar   d. membranophone

_d_ 5. African hand drum

_c_ 6. gong

Complete the following questions.

7. In which instrument category do horns and flutes fall? _aerophone_

8. The instrument category that produces sound from the substance of the instrument as it is rubbed, struck, or shaken is _membranophone_

9. _idiophone_ describes any instrument that is sounded from a tightly stretched skin that is struck, rubbed, or plucked.

10. _Chordophone_ describes an instrument that produces sound from a vibrating string stretched between two points. It can be sounded by two means: _bowing_ and _plucking_ .

11. Name two modern Western instruments of Middle Eastern origin:

   a. _acoustic guitar_ b. _electric guitar_
                                          timpani

True or False

_F_ 12. The gong is widely used throughout Africa.

_T_ 13. Members of the xylophone family are used in Southeast Asia and Africa.

_T_ 14. Trumpets and horns were used in the ancient world.

_F_ 15. The tom-tom is a type of gong of African origin.

_T_ 16. Chamber groups combining strings and percussion are common in India.

_T_ 17. The gamelan is a type of orchestra in Indonesia.

F 18. Gagaku is the name of an African drum.

T 19. Turkish Janissary bands made use of wind and percussion instruments.

F 20. All ensembles around the world make use of a conductor.

T 21. In some cultures, women's voices are preferred for certain styles of music.

T 22. The sitar is used in classical music from India.

T 23. Music serves different functions in different societies.

F 24. Musical genres, or categories of music, are the same in all societies.

T 25. Vocal timbre, or tone quality, varies from culture to culture, based on differing preferences.

F 26. In modern times, all music is notated, or written down.

T 27. Oral transmission involves performance without notation.

F 28. Classical (art) music is never influenced by traditional or popular music.

T 29. Crossover refers to a kind of music notation.

iMusic Listening (Student Resource Disc)

Simple Gifts

30. What order of voice parts do you hear entering in this choral folk song setting?

___ ABTS ___ TSAB X SATB

Bhimpalási

31. Check all the categories of music instruments you hear in this example:

___ aerophone X chordophone ___ idiophone

X membranophone

Dougla Dance

32. Check all the categories of world music instruments you hear:

___ aerophone ___ chordophone ___ idiophone

___ membranophone

El Cihualteco

33. Check all the categories of world music instruments you hear:

___ aerophone ___ chordophone ___ idiophone

___ membranophone

7. *Review* Western Orchestral Instruments
Chap. 8

Exercises

Identify each of the instruments pictured below in four ways: ts name, chosen from column I; its instrument family, from column II; its n ans of sound production, from column III; and its world instrument category from column IV.

I. INSTRUMENT
  a. bassoon
  b. clarinet
  c. double bass
  d. flute
  e. French horn
  f. oboe
  g. saxophone
  h. timpani
  i. trombone
  j. trumpet
  k. tuba
  l. violin

II. FAMILY
  m. brass
  n. percussion
  o. strings
  p. woodwinds

III. SOUND PRODUCTION
  q. blown double reed
  r. blown single reed
  s. bowed string
  t. struck with mallets
  u. air column divided across hole
  v. lips buzzing into mouthpiece

IV. CATE ORY
  w. aer phones
  x. cho ophones
  y. idio ones
  z. men ranophones

(Sample)

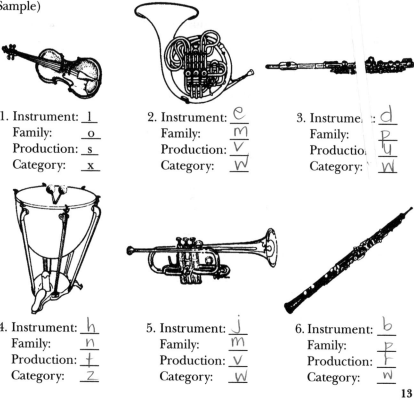

1. Instrument: _l_
   Family: _o_
   Production: _s_
   Category: _x_

2. Instrument: _e_
   Family: _m_
   Production: _v_
   Category: _w_

3. Instrume   : _d_
   Family: _p_
   Productio: _u_
   Category: _w_

4. Instrument: _h_
   Family: _n_
   Production: _t_
   Category: _z_

5. Instrument: _j_
   Family: _m_
   Production: _v_
   Category: _w_

6. Instrument: _b_
   Family: _p_
   Production: _r_
   Category: _w_

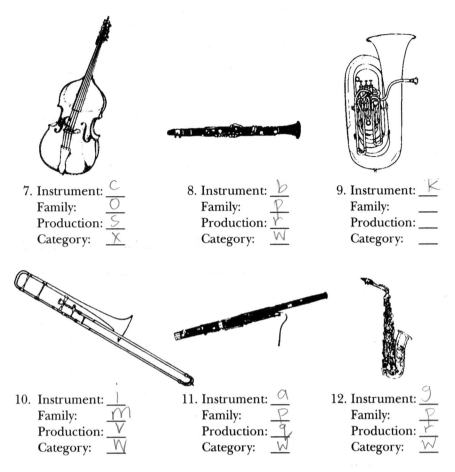

7. Instrument: C
   Family: O
   Production: S
   Category: X

8. Instrument: b
   Family: P
   Production: r
   Category: W

9. Instrument: K
   Family: __
   Production: __
   Category: __

10. Instrument: l
    Family: M
    Production: V
    Category: W

11. Instrument: a
    Family: P
    Production: q
    Category: W

12. Instrument: g
    Family: P
    Production: r
    Category: W

iMusic Listening (Student Resource Disc)

Identify the specific instrument (or Western instrument family) heard in each example below.

13. *Greensleeves* Instrument: _____guitar_____

14. Bach: *Jesu, Joy of Man's Desiring* Instrument: _____organ_____

15. Haydn: *Emperor* Quartet Family: _____String_____

16. *The Star-Spangled Banner* two families: _____Brass_____ and percussion

17. Mendelssohn: *Spring Song* Instrument: _____Piano_____

18. Bach: Sarabande Instrument: _____Cello_____

19. Sousa: *Stars and Stripes Forever*, Trio
    Countermelody instrument: _____Brass, percussion, woodwinds_____

20. Minuet in D minor (*Anna Magdalena Notebook*)
    Instrument: _____Harpsichord_____

21. Mouret: Rondeau, from *Suite de symphonies*
    Melody instrument: _____Violin_____

14

> ## 8. *Review* Musical Instruments and Ensembles
> Chaps. 7–9

Terms to Remember

a cappella	duo sonata	pitch
alto	duration	pitched
baritone	embouchure	plucked
bass	jazz band	register
baton	madrigal choir	soprano
bowed	mezzo-soprano	string quartet
brass quintet	orchestra	synthesizer
chamber music	organ	tenor
chorus	part songs	timbre
concert band	piano trio	unpitched
concert master	piano quartet	volume
conductor	piano quintet	woodwind quintet

Exercises

Complete the following questions.

1. The four qualities of any musical sound are ___pitch___, ___duration___, ___volume___, and ___timbre___.

2. The distinctive sound of each instrument is its ___timbre___.

3. List the three standard voice parts for women (highest to lowest).
   ___soprano___   ___mezzo-soprano___   ___alto___

4. List the three standard voice parts for men (highest to lowest).
   ___tenor___   ___baritone___   ___bass___

5. The two categories of orchestral string instruments, grouped by the way they are played, are ___bowed___ and ___plucked___.
   Name an instrument from each: ___violin___ and ___guitar___

6. The two categories of percussion instruments are ___pitched___ and ___unpitched___.
   Give an example of each: ___timpani___ and ___snare drum___

7. The lips, lower facial muscles, and jaw are referred to as a wind player's ___embouchure___.

8. _A cappella_ refers to music sung without instrumental accompaniment.

9. The _piano_ is an instrument that produces sound via a keyboard mechanism that causes hammers to strike strings.

10. Which keyboard instrument produces sound from air flowing through its many pipes? _organ_

11. Small ensembles with one musician per part play _chamber music_

12. The standard ensemble consisting of 2 violins, 1 viola, and 1 cello is known as a(n) _string quartet_.

13. A chamber ensemble that includes flute, oboe, clarinet, French horn, and bassoon is known as a(n) _woodwind quintet_

14. Name a chamber ensemble of piano and strings. _piano trio_
piano quartet
piano quintet

Match the following string effects with their definitions.

_c_ 15. pizzicato
_a_ 16. trill
_g_ 17. vibrato
_b_ 18. muting
_f_ 19. staccato
_d_ 20. double stopping
_e_ 21. glissando

a. a rapid alternation between a tone and the one above it

b. muffling the sound with a small attachment on the bridge

c. plucking the string with the finger

d. playing two notes at one time

e. a slide on the string while bowing

f. a short, detached style of playing

g. a throbbing effect produced by wiggling the finger slightly while bowing

iMusic Listening (Student Resource Disc)

22. *Joy to the World*   Ensemble: _chorus_

23. *When the Saints Go Marching In*   Ensemble: _choir_

24. Josquin: *El grillo*   Ensemble: _chamber choir_

25. Sousa: *Stars and Stripes Forever*   Ensemble: _symphony orchestra_

26. Haydn: *Military* Symphony   Ensemble: _symphony orchestra_

27. Hildegard: Kyrie   Ensemble: _madrigal choir_

28. Reicha: Woodwind Quintet   Name the instruments in the order you hear them:

Bassoon, Clarinet, Flute, Oboe, French horn

16

> **9. *Listen* Britten's *The Young Person's Guide to the Orchestra***
> LG 1

Exercises

Locate the recording of *The Young Person's Guide to the Orchestra* on your Student
Resource Disc. Follow Listening Guide 1 in your text while listening, then
answer the questions below.

THEME

1. What was Britten's source for the theme (main melody) of this work?

   Purcell : Rondeau

2. What instruments are heard in the original version of the theme?

   (Note: The original version is in your iMusic examples as well.)

   violins, viola, cello, double bass

3. Describe the character of the theme in your own words.
   I believe this would be
   Strong, colorful. considered the genre to
   symphony because it consists of a four-movement orchestral
4. How does the composer firmly establish this melody for the listener?   _work._

   Repition of the melody six times

5. Can you differentiate between the sounds of each instrument family?

   yes Describe in your own words the timbre or distinctive sound

   of each family below. _cheerful/soft/Fmajor (high)_
   Woodwinds: _wind hole or reeded instruments/soft_
   commanding E-flat major (lower)
   Brass: _vibrating lips and airforce/moderate_
   Strings: _bowed Gm to Dm_
   Percussion: _struck powerful/deep/loud_

VARIATIONS

After the statements of the theme (principal melody) by each instrument
family, Britten begins a series of variations on the theme.

6. How would you define a variation of a given melody?

   The different instruments & their accompaniments

7. Can you recognize the theme throughout the variations? _no_

8. Can you distinguish the solo instrument over those that are playing the

   accompaniment? _yes, each variation is lead by a_
   single instrument accompanied by
   various others   **17**

9. Which woodwind instruments do you find easy to identify?

oboes, flutes, clarinets, bassoon

Which are difficult? piccolos

10. Which string instruments do you find easy to identify?

Violins

Which are difficult? viola, cello

11. Which brass instruments do you find easy to identify?

trumpet, tuba

Which are difficult? trombones, frenchhorns

12. Of the percussion instruments heard, which have a definite pitch?

Timpani

Which are unpitched? snare drum, tambourines

FUGUE

Use the last section of the work as a final review of the instruments. Here each instrument is heard playing a very quick statement of a new theme or melody.

13. Knowing the range an instrument plays in will help you distinguish it from other family members whose timbres are similar. Arrange the instruments of each family from highest to lowest, as they are heard in both the variations and the fugue. Assign number 1 to the highest family member, 2 to the next highest, and so on.

4 bassoon	6: 2 viola	9 2 French horn
1 piccolo	7 3 cello	12 4 tuba
3 clarinet	5 1 violin	10 1 trumpet
2 flute	8 4 double bass	11 3 trombone

14. How does Britten use imitation in this section of the piece?

Fragments of the theme are added as each instrument enters accordingly

15. Where is the climax of the work? The four families combine to create a single unit sound called the symphony orchestra

18

> **10.** *Review* **Style and Function in Music**
> **Chap.** 10

Exercises

Complete the following questions.

59 1. What does the term "genre" mean? *categories of repertory*

     59 Name a literary genre (e.g., short story). *Fire + Ice by Robert Frost*

     59 Name a musical genre. *symphony*

59 2. What distinguishes sacred music from secular music?

sacred music is for spiritual and religious functions; while secular music is for and about everyday people outside religion

3. What determines the style of any work of art?

The genre, form, and medium determine the style of any work of art.

4. Specifically, what determines the style of a musical work?

A musical style is created through individual treatment of the elements (melody, rhythm, harmony, texture, form dynamics, and tempo).

63-65 5. What are some factors that may make certain styles of non-Western music sound different or unfamiliar to Westerners?

_____

_____

_____

6. Style is also what makes popular music sound different from classical music. List some categories of popular music that you think represent differing styles.

jazz, rock, blues, metal, pop, + rap

_____

_____

7. Place the following Western style periods in chronological order by numbering them from 1 (the earliest) to 6 (the latest) in the left column. Give the approximate dates of each era in the right column.

	ERA	DATES
3	Baroque	1600 – 1750
1	Middle Ages	400 – 1450
5	Romantic	1820 – 1900
6	Twentieth century	1900 – present
4	Classical	1750 – 1825
2	Renaissance	1450 – 1600

iMusic Listening (Student Resource Disc)

8. Listen to these two orchestral examples from different musical periods. Describe the stylistic differences you hear.

Catán: Interlude from *Rappaccini's Daughter* and Mozart: Symphony No. 40, III

Late 20th century / Classical

Answer questions 9–13 about the following composition title:

Ludwig van Beethoven: Piano Sonata in C minor, Op. 13 (*Pathétique*)

9. The name of the composer is Ludwig van Beethoven.

10. Which word tells us the performing medium? Pathétique

11. What is the genre for the work? Piano Sonata

12. What is the catalogue number for the work? Op. 13

13. What is the descriptive title (or nickname) for the work?
Piano sonata in C minor, Op. 13

> **11. *Explore* The Roles of Music around the World**
> CP 2

Exercises

Complete the following questions.

1. Name some activities that might be performed while singing work songs.

   Mining, rail road building, field work (slavery)

2. Describe the responsorial singing style of work songs.

   _____

   _____

3. From what type of work song did blues and spirituals develop?

   Blues and spirituals grew out of the field
   hollers of slaves brought to the U.S. from
   West Africa

4. Can you name a folk song that might have originally been a work song?

   "Ive been working on the railroad"

5. What are some common traits of lullabies around the world?

   Sang in the vernacular, often repetitive, slowly
   paced, and share great rhythmic motion, and often
   passed down through oral transmission.

6. What is a vocable? _____

7. In which meter are Western lullabies most often set? _____

   Why? _____

8. Name a lullaby that you have heard. _____

9. How is music used in worship services and what is its function?

   _____

   _____

10. Give examples of instruments or ensembles used to accompany

    military troops. _____

    _____

    _____

11. What is the name of the bugle call used to wake up the troops?

    _____ Have you heard this bugle call? _____ If so,

    where?_____

iMusic Listening Assignment (Student Resource Disc)

Listen to the following selections and describe the characteristics and possible use of each below:

Sleep Song (Hopi lullaby)
Battle Hymn of the Republic (Civil War song)
Swing Low, Sweet Chariot (African-American spiritual)

Or visit StudySpace (www.wwnorton.com/enjoy), read this Cultural Perspective, and follow links provided there. Write an essay describing your online research.

_____

_____

_____

_____

_____

_____

_____

_____

_____

_____

_____

_____

_____

_____

_____

_____

_____

_____

_____

_____

_____

_____

_____

_____

_____

12. *Review* Music in the Middle Ages
Chaps. 11–13

Exercises

SACRED MUSIC

True or False

_____ 1. Medieval monasteries played a central role in the preservation of knowledge from earlier times.

_____ 2. The church was especially important in shaping secular music of early times.

_____ 3. Hildegard of Bingen was an abbess who wrote church music.

_____ 4. Much music is left to us today from Greek and Roman civilizations.

_____ 5. Charlemagne was an early Roman Catholic pope who encouraged singing in the church.

_____ 6. Early musical notation, called neumes, developed as a memory tool for singers who learned chants orally.

_____ 7. The chants of the church used only the major and minor scale patterns found in later music.

_____ 8. The Mass of the Roman Catholic Church is celebrated daily and includes the Proper, which is appropriate to that feast, and the Ordinary, which remains the same for all feast days.

_____ 9. The Notre Dame School is renowned for early polyphonic writing called organum.

_____ 10. Léonin and Pérotin are important composers from the St. Peter's School of organum in Rome.

_____ 11. The cloistered life in the Middle Ages was open only to men.

_____ 12. People who entered religious orders led a demanding lifestyle.

Complete the following sentences.

13. The _____ is the most solemn service of the Roman Catholic Church. How often is it celebrated? _____

14. The _____ are a series of services celebrated in religious institutions at various hours of the day.

15. The body of music for the Roman Catholic Church in the Middle Ages is generally called _____.

16. Medieval scale patterns used in Western music are called _____.

17. Music performed with exchanges between a soloist and chorus is said to be _____.

18. The language of the early church, also used by scholars, was _____.

SECULAR MUSIC

Match the following groups of musicians with their descriptions below.

_____ 19. trouvères   a. female poet-musicians from France

_____ 20. troubadours   b. poet-musicians of northern France

_____ 21. jongleurs   c. German singers of courtly love

_____ 22. trobairitz   d. poet-musicians of southern France

_____ 23. Minnesingers   e. wandering actor-singers

Multiple Choice

_____ 24. The music of the troubadours and trouvères included:
   a. laments and love songs.
   b. political and war songs.
   c. dance songs.
   d. all of the above.

_____ 25. Which was NOT an activity associated with secular music in medieval society?
   a. dancing and dinner entertainment
   b. devotional services
   c. jousts and tournaments
   d. military and civic events

_____ 26. Which factor did NOT contribute significantly to the rise in the status of women in the Middle Ages?
   a. the cults of Marian worship
   b. the age of chivalry
   c. the love songs of court minstrels
   d. the attitudes of feudal society

27. What were the principal values during the age of chivalry? Which of these are valid today?

_____

_____

28. Cite a popular song of today that echoes the sentiments of unrequited love heard in medieval songs.

_____

_____

---

13. *Explore* **Chant as Music for Worship**
CP 3

Exercises

Complete the following questions.

1. How would you characterize chant musically? _____

    _____

2. How are the performances of the psalms similar in the early Judaic and

    the early Christian traditions? _____

    _____

    What is a cantor?_____

3. How are the sacred texts of the Koran presented in worship?

    _____

*4. How do the chants for private devotion and public performance differ

    in Islamic worship? _____

    _____

*5. What is unusual about the vocal style of Tibetan chant? _____

    _____

    Which ensemble has popularized this style around the world?

    _____

    Which album by this group was recorded during a U.S. tour?

    _____

*6. What is the acoustical meaning of the term "fundamental"?

    _____

7. Describe the Afro-Cuban religion of Santería. (You may wish to read

    more about this topic online.) _____

    _____

    _____

    _____

    _____

iMusic Listening Assignment (Student Resource Disc)

Listen to the following two iMusic examples of chant and discuss their musical style below.

Hildegard: Kyrie and *Osain* (Cuban Santería)

Or visit StudySpace (www.wwnorton.com/enjoy), read this Cultural Perspective, and follow links provided there. Write an essay describing your online research.

> ### 14. *Listen* Hildegard of Bingen and Chant
> *Gregorian Chant: Kyrie (**LG** 2, *e***LG**)
> Hildegard of Bingen: *Alleluia, O virga mediatrix* (**LG** 3, **Sh** 2, *e***LG**)

Exercises

Describe the musical characteristics of Gregorian chant:

1. Texture: _____

2. Rhythm/meter: _____

3. Type of movement: _____

4. Range: _____

5. Scale pattern: _____

6. From which service in the liturgy is the Kyrie? _____

7. What are the notational symbols for chant called? _____

Match the text setting terms with their correct definitions.

_____ 8. syllabic   a. many notes per syllable

_____ 9. neumatic   b. one note per syllable

_____ 10. melismatic   c. syllabic style with short melismas of 5 to 6 notes

*Listen to the Gregorian chant Kyrie while following the Listening Guide, then answer questions 11–16.

11. The Kyrie is a part of the ___ Ordinary or ___ Proper of the Mass.

12. The text of the Kyrie is based on a _____ prayer.

13. The Kyrie consists of _____ phrases sung _____ times each.

14. The Kyrie is sung in a _____ style, alternating

     between a _____ and a _____.

15. The melody is ___ conjunct or ___ disjunct and wavelike with a

     ___ small, ___ medium, or ___ large range that grows ___ wider or

     ___ narrower in the second and third sections.

16. The text setting (relationship of notes to words) alternates between

     _____ and _____.

Listen to Hildegard of Bingen's *Alleluia, O virga mediatrix* while following the Listening Guide, then answer questions 17–25.

17. For which liturgical occasion(s) was Hildegard's chant *Alleluia, O virga mediatrix* sung? _____

18. Who is praised in the text? _____

19. This chant is sung in alternation between a soloist and a chorus; this style is known as _____.

Multiple Choice

_____ 20. Which term best describes the texture?
     a. monophonic
     b. polyphonic
     c. homophonic

_____ 21. Which best describes the melodic movement of Hildegard's chant?
     a. completely conjunct
     b. mostly conjunct with a few leaps
     c. very disjunct

_____ 22. Which best describes the text setting in *Alleluia, O virga mediatrix?*
     a. all syllabic
     b. mostly neumatic
     c. mostly melismatic

23. What musical characteristic(s) heard in this chant could be considered unique to the music of Hildegard?

_____

_____

Cite an example in the chant where this characteristic is heard.

_____

24. Cite a specific example of word painting in *Alleluia, O virga mediatrix.* What is the text (and translation) and how does Hildegard depict the word musically?

_____

_____

25. What unique qualities did Hildegard possess that made her famous in her day?

_____

_____

_____

_____

15. *Listen* Organum and Motet

Notre Dame School Organum: *Gaude Maria virgo* (**LG** 4, Sh 3, *e***LG**)
*Anonymous: *Mout me fu grief/Robin m'aime/Portare* (**LG** 5, *e***LG**)

Exercises

Listen to the Notre Dame School Organum *Gaude Maria virgo* while following the Listening Guide, then answer questions 1–12.

1. The earliest type of polyphony is called _____.

2. Polyphony brought about the use of _____, in which

   different voices sing together.

3. Composers of organum based their compositions on _____

   _____.

4. Name two composers associated with the Notre Dame School.

   _____ and _____

   Where was this school of composition located? _____

   In which century(centuries) did it flourish? _____

5. Which composer is credited with writing the *Great Book of Organum*?

   _____

6. Which composer is sometimes credited with writing the organum

   Gaude Maria virgo?_____

7. The text of *Gaude Maria virgo* is in praise of _____

   and would be sung for occasions celebrating _____.

8. The text setting alternates between _____ and

   _____, with _____ (how many?) voices singing

   rhythmically over a sustained bottom voice.

9. The bottom voice sings the _____ part in long notes.

10. The texture shifts from _____ at the beginning to

    _____.

11. The upper voices feature a repeated rhythmic pattern known as a

    _____.

    Describe the pattern you hear. _____

29

12. Can you hear the two moving upper parts? _____ How would you describe how they move? _____

Can you hear the lowest voice? _____ Is it easy or difficult to pick out? _____

*Listen to the anonymous motet *Mout me fu grief/Robin m'aime/Portare* while following the Listening Guide, then answer questions 13–27.

True or False

____ 13. The texture of this work is monophonic.

____ 14. The genre of this work is a secular motet.

____ 15. The upper voices sing the same text but in different languages.

____ 16. The texts are based on French love poems.

____ 17. The bottom voice is newly composed, with no pre-existent musical basis.

____ 18. The tenor voice was often performed instrumentally.

____ 19. This motet is in quadruple meter.

____ 20. The middle line is a trouvère love song.

____ 21. The upper voices have simple rhythms that move as slowly as the tenor voice.

22. Describe briefly the origin of the motet. _____

_____

_____

23. What are the typical languages for motet texts? _____

24. Explain the term "polytextual" as it applies to the motet.

_____

_____

*25. What is the subject of the top voice (triplum) text in this motet?

_____

*26. What is the subject of the middle voice (duplum) text?

_____

*27. What is the term for the bottom voice in a motet? _____

What is the derivation of this word? _____

16. *Listen* Medieval Secular Music
Raimbaut de Vaqueiras: *Kalenda maya* (**LG** 6, Sh 4, *e***LG**)
Machaut: *Puis qu'en oubli* (**LG** 7, Sh 5, *e***LG**)

Exercises

Listen to the dance song *Kalenda maya* while following the Listening Guide, then answer questions 1–8.

1. The composer of this song was a(n):
   ___ troubadour ___ trouvère ___ goliard

2. The song tells of:
   ___ a crusader's battles ___ courtly love ___ political issues

3. This song is a French dance known as the:
   ___ saltarello ___ estampie ___ ronde

4. The melodic structure for one verse is cast in:
   ___ two ___ three ___ four sections.

5. The overall form is considered:
   ___ strophic ___ through-composed ___ ternary

6. The string instrument heard in this performance is a:
   ___ pipe ___ harp ___ rebec

7. The poet has addressed this poem to:
   ___ his ruler ___ a courtly lady ___ the pope

8. The meter featured in this dance is: ___ duple ___ triple ___ compound

Listen to the Machaut chanson *Puis qu'en oubli* while following the Listening Guide, then answer questions 9–22.

9. This work represents: ___ secular music ___ sacred music

10. The era it represents is: ___ Ars antiqua ___ Ars nova

11. The chanson's texture is: ___ monophonic ___ polyphonic

12. The chanson's structure is: ___ a fixed form ___ freely composed

13. The chanson's text tells of: ___ unrequited love ___ praise of the Virgin Mary

14. The repeated text and music is called: ___ verse ___ refrain

15. In which form is this chanson? ___ ballade ___ rondeau

16. The setting is for: ___ three low voices ___ mixed men's and women's voices

31

17. How many different musical sections are heard? ___ two ___ three

18. The meter of the chanson is: ___ duple ___ triple

19. The composer was: ___ a troubadour ___ a courtier and cleric

20. What accounts for the complexity you hear in this work?

_____

_____

21. What holds the work together structurally? _____

_____

_____

22. Describe the sentiment of courtly love expressed in the text.

_____

_____

_____

EARLY INSTRUMENTS

____ 23. Which string instrument is featured at the beginning of the dance
        Kalenda maya?
        a. harp
        b. lute
        c. rebec

____ 24. The tabor is a:
        a. brass instrument.
        b. percussion instrument.
        c. woodwind instrument.

____ 25. Instruments used for outdoor events were:
        a. *bas* (soft)
        b. *haut* (loud)
        c. *grand* (large)

26. Which early instruments have modern counterparts? Which do not?

_____

_____

_____

_____

---

17. *Explore* **Opening Doors to the East**
CP 4

Exercises

Complete the following questions.

1. What was the purpose of the Crusades? _____

   _____

   In which centuries did they take place? _____

2. What modern geographical locale was the goal of the crusaders?

   _____

3. What military skills did Europeans learn from their enemies?

   _____

4. What types of knowledge were acquired from the Arab world?

   _____

   _____

5. Name three ways in which music was influenced by the Eastern world
   during the crusades:

   a. _____

   b. _____

   c. _____

6. What Chinese ruler welcomed Marco Polo into his empire?

   _____ In which century? _____

*7. What technical skills did Marco Polo and his explorers bring to western
    Europe from China? _____

    _____

*8. What can we deduce from Polo's writings about the Tartars' use of
    music? _____

    _____

iMusic Listening Assignment (Student Resource Disc)

Listen to the following selections and describe the sound of the instruments and styles from the ancient trade route known as the Silk Road. Try to use technical music terms you have learned to describe the style.

  Middle Eastern music: *Avaz of Bayate Esfahan* (Iran)
  Asian music: *In a Mountain Path* (China)

Or visit StudySpace (www.wwnorton.com/enjoy), read this Cultural Perspective, and follow links provided there. Write an essay describing your online research.

_____

_____

_____

_____

_____

_____

_____

_____

_____

_____

_____

_____

_____

_____

_____

_____

_____

_____

_____

_____

_____

_____

_____

_____

_____

---

18. *Review* **The Renaissance Spirit**
Chap. 14

Exercises

Check a or b for each.

1. The Renaissance represents:
___ a. a sudden rebirth in learning and the arts
___ b. an increased awareness of the cultures of learned civilizations

2. The new era was characterized by:
___ a. an increased secular orientation
___ b. an increased religious orientation

3. The Renaissance was an age of:
___ a. scientific and intellectual inquiry
___ b. acceptance of faith and authority

4. This era found inspiration in:
___ a. the culture of the early Christian Church
___ b. the cultures of ancient Greece and Rome

5. Check all those historical events that took place during the Renaissance.
___ a. the discovery of the New World
___ b. the invention of printing
___ c. the writing of the Magna Carta
___ d. the fall of the Roman Empire
___ e. the Protestant Reformation
___ f. the writing of the U.S. Constitution

6. Match the following well-known Renaissance personalities with their descriptions.

____ Michelangelo   a. Italian scientist and astronomer

____ Machiavelli   b. Italian statesman

____ Galileo   c. Italian painter and sculptor

____ Martin Luther   d. English playwright

____ Shakespeare   e. German religious reformer

7. Name two great artists and a work of art created by each during the Renaissance. (Check text illustrations for examples.)

ARTIST   WORK OF ART

_____   _____

_____   _____

8. The means by which musicians made their living in the Renaissance are similar to today's. For each of the following supporting institutions, list one specific use of music in the Renaissance and a parallel activity today.

	RENAISSANCE	MODERN DAY
Church:	_____	_____
Civic:	_____	_____
Amateur music-making:	_____	_____
Aristocratic courts:	_____	_____

9. What effect did the rise of a new middle class of merchants have on the commerce of music?

_____

_____

10. What roles did women play in music during the Renaissance era?

_____

_____

RENAISSANCE MUSICAL STYLE

True or False

____ 11. The Renaissance saw the rise of solo instrumental music alongside the great vocal forms.

____ 12. An *a cappella* performance of a vocal work might feature improvised instrumental accompaniment.

____ 13. The predominant texture of Renaissance vocal music was imitative polyphony.

____ 14. Expressive musical devices were frequently linked to the text in Renaissance music.

____ 15. The use of a cantus firmus, or fixed melody, was abandoned in the Renaissance in favor of freer forms.

____ 16. Renaissance music reflected a new taste for duple meter.

____ 17. Renaissance music is characterized by the empty sonorities of open fourths and fifths.

> **19. *Explore* Mythology in Music and Art**
> CP 5

Exercises

Complete the following questions.

1. Who is the ancient god(dess) of:

    love: _____

    luck: _____

    beauty: _____

2. What do the Muses do? _____

    _____

    Name several of them: _____

3. In the famous painting *The Birth of Venus* by Botticelli (see text, p. 98), why is the goddess on a shell? Read about her online to answer this.

    _____

    _____

4. In ancient mythology, what was Apollo's instrument?_____

    What was Pan's instrument? _____

    Where can these instruments be heard today? _____

    What was the result of their famous contest? _____

    _____

*5. What is the quadrivium? _____

    How does this relate to your general studies today? _____

    _____

*6. From whose ancient Roman writing is the story of the musical *My Fair Lady* drawn? _____ On which more modern play is it based? _____

Essay

Choose one of the topics below, research it online, and write an essay detailing your findings.

1. Isabella d'Este and her role as a patroness of music
2. Music in Shakespeare's plays
3. The views of music held by the ancient philosophers Plato and Aristotle

Or visit StudySpace (www.wwnorton.com/enjoy), read this Cultural Perspective, and follow links provided there. Write an essay describing your online research.

---

20. *Review* Music in the Renaissance Era
Chaps. 15–16

Exercises

SACRED MUSIC

Multiple Choice

_____ 1. Which genre of music was generally NOT sung in the Roman
Catholic Church?
a. chansons
b. motets
c. Masses

_____ 2. Which of the following makes up the Ordinary of the Mass?
a. Introit, Gradual, Communion, Ite missa est
b. Kyrie, Gloria, Credo, Sanctus, Agnus Dei, Ite missa est
c. Kyrie, Gloria, Collect, Epistle, Gradual, Canon

_____ 3. Which of the following movements of the Mass have three-part text
and musical structures?
a. Kyrie and Gloria
b. Sanctus and Agnus Dei
c. Kyrie and Agnus Dei

_____ 4. Which of the following characteristics is NOT typical of the
Renaissance motet?
a. multi-voiced, sometimes based on a chant
b. Latin texts, often in praise of the Virgin Mary
c. monophonic, and sung in the vernacular

_____ 5. Which of the following was NOT recommended by the Council of Trent?
a. remove secularisms from church music
b. use more instruments in church music
c. make the words more understandable

_____ 6. The Catholic Church's reform movement toward piety was:
a. the Reformation.
b. the Counter-Reformation.
c. the Ordinary.

True or False

_____ *7. Du Fay used cantus firmus technique in his Masses.

_____ 8. Josquin spent his entire productive career in northern Europe.

_____ 9. Palestrina's patrons included several popes.

_____ 10. Palestrina was a Burgundian composer.

_____ 11. Renaissance composers often set the Ordinary of the Mass
polyphonically.

True or False

_____ 12. The principal forms of Renaissance secular music were the chanson and the motet.

_____ 13. Women were barred from secular music-making in the Renaissance.

_____ 14. The madrigal flourished principally in France.

_____ 15. The English madrigal was generally more serious and complex than its Italian counterpart.

_____ 16. The texts of the chanson and the madrigal dealt largely with love, both courtly and rustic, and were written in the vernacular (language of the people).

_____ 17. Instrumental music-making was a feature of home life.

_____ 18. Instruments were used exclusively for the dance and never with voices in the Renaissance.

_____ 19. Specific instruments were rarely called for in Renaissance music.

_____ 20. Instruments were divided into loud and soft categories, their use determined by the occasion.

_____ 21. Monteverdi contributed significantly to the development of the Italian madrigal.

_____ 22. Word painting is an expressive feature used in madrigals.

*Match the dance types below with their correct descriptions.

_____ 23. pavane   a. an Italian jumping dance

_____ 24. galliard   b. a German dance in moderate duple meter

_____ 25. allemande   c. a slow, stately processional dance

_____ 26. saltarello   d. a quick French dance

27. What was the *Concerto delle donne*?

_____

28. What was new and remarkable about their singing style?

_____

_____

_____

29. How did the tastes of the English composers differ from those of the Italians in selecting madrigal texts? _____

_____

---

21. *Listen* Renaissance Sacred Music
*Du Fay: *L'homme armé* Mass, Kyrie (**LG** 8, *e***LG**)
Josquin: *Ave Maria . . . virgo serena* (**LG** 9, Sh 6, *e***LG**)
Palestrina: *Pope Marcellus* Mass, Gloria (**LG** 10, Sh 7, *e***LG**)

Exercises

*Listen to the early-Renaissance Mass movement by Du Fay, then answer questions 1–9.

1. For how many voice parts is this Mass set? _____

2. The Kyrie is the first musical movement of the _____ of the Mass.

3. What is the cantus firmus (fixed song) on which this Mass is set?

   _____

   Can you hear the cantus firmus in the work? _____

4. What is the overall form of the movement? _____

5. How does the text shape the form? _____

   _____

6. What is the predominant texture of the movement? _____

   _____

7. In which meter is this movement set? _____

8. Does the harmony sound hollow or full? _____

9. Why did the Catholic Church object to masses such as this one later in the sixteenth century?

   _____

   _____

Listen to the Josquin motet while following the Listening Guide, then answer questions 10–18.

10. For how many voices is this work set? _____

11. Whose virtues are praised in its text? _____

12. Describe the structure of the text. _____

   _____

13. In which language is the text written? _____

14. What textures does Josquin employ to set off the different sections of

   the text? _____

41

15. Is this work _____ based on a chant or _____ freely composed?
    Explain. _____

    _____

16. Does this recording use _____ male voices only or _____ mixed voices?
    What voices would have been used in the Renaissance? _____

17. Is this work performed _____ *a cappella* or _____ with accompaniment?

18. Would you say that Josquin's first priority was the music or the text in this
    work? _____ Explain your answer. _____

    _____

Listen to the Palestrina Mass movement while following the Listening Guide,
then answer questions 19–29.

19. Is this movement part of the Mass _____ Ordinary or _____ Proper?

20. For how many voice parts is the Mass written? _____

21. How does Palestrina create contrast in the voices and ranges?

    _____

    _____

22. Was this Mass originally sung by ____ male voices or ____ mixed voices?
    Explain. _____

    _____

23. Is this work performed _____ *a cappella* or _____ with instruments?

24. Is its harmony best described as _____ consonant or _____ dissonant?

25. Is its texture more _____ homophonic or _____ polyphonic?

26. Is its meter _____ duple or _____ triple?

27. How does Palestrina make the text clear and audible? _____

    _____

28. What musical concerns of the Council of Trent did Palestrina try to
    accommodate in this work? _____

    _____

29. Comparing this work to the Josquin motet *Ave Maria . . . virgo serena,*
    which sounds more modern to you? _____
    Explain your answer. _____

    _____

---

22. *Listen* Sixteenth-Century Secular Music
*Josquin: *Mille regretz* (**LG** 11, *e***LG**)
 Susato: Three Dances (**LG** 12, Sh 8, *e***LG**)
 Monteverdi: *Ecco mormorar l'onde* (**LG** 13, Sh 9, *e***LG**)
 Farmer: *Fair Phyllis* (**LG** 14, Sh 10, *e***LG**)

Exercises

*Listen to the Josquin chanson *Mille regretz* while following the Listening Guide, then answer questions 1–3.

1. In which language is Josquin's *Mille regretz* set? _____

2. What is the subject of its text? _____

_____

3. What makes this chanson sound sad and archaic? _____

_____

Listen to the Three Dances by Susato while following the Listening Guide, then answer questions 4–7.

4. Which group of instruments are featured in our performance of these

   dances? _____ *haut* or _____ *bas* Explain what these categories mean.

   _____

   _____

   _____

5. What kind of dance is a ronde? _____

6. What is the form of each of these three dances? _____

7. What instrument is featured at the beginning of the second ronde?

   _____

THE MADRIGAL

Listen to Monteverdi's madrigal *Ecco mormorar l'onde* while following the Listening Guide in the text, then answer questions 8–12.

8. In which country did the madrigal originate? _____

9. Cite a clear example of word painting in this Monteverdi madrigal.

   _____

   _____

   _____

10. How does the mood change as the madrigal progresses?

_____

_____

11. For how many voice parts is Monteverdi's *Ecco mormorar l'onde* written?

_____ Do all the voices sing all the time? _____

12. Where does this work fall in the output of madrigals by Monteverdi?

_____

Listen to Farmer's madrigal *Fair Phyllis* while following the Listening Guide in the text, then answer questions 14–19.

13. For how many voice parts is *Fair Phyllis* written? _____

Which parts? _____

14. Cite an example of clear word painting in *Fair Phyllis*.

_____

_____

_____

15. Describe why this madrigal might be considered rustic or pastoral.

_____

_____

16. Listen for the brief change to triple meter in *Fair Phyllis*. What is its musical effect? _____

17. How did the English madrigal differ from the Italian madrigal?

_____

_____

_____

18. Consider a contemporary love song (a ballad, a Broadway musical selection, or a rock song). Describe below how the musical style supports the text. Are there examples of word painting in the modern piece?

Selection: _____

Description: _____

_____

_____

_____

---

23. *Review* Transition to the Baroque
Trans. I
*Gabrieli: *O quam suavis* (**LG** 15, *e***LG**)

Exercises

Fill in the answers below.

1. Giovanni Gabrieli was active as a composer at St. Mark's in the city of

    _____.

2. One important characteristic of music at St. Mark's was the use of two

    or three choirs, called _____ singing.

3. The use of these choirs in alternation and then together is a singing

    style known as _____.

4. This style marked a change from the predominantly polyphonic texture

    of the Renaissance to a more _____ texture, in which

    the words could be understood better.

For each of the traits listed below, indicate with the appropriate letter the
style to which it relates.

    a. Renaissance style
    b. Baroque style

____   5. precise instruments specified

____   6. modal harmony predominant

____   7. *a cappella* vocal performance

____   8. solo singing (monody) prevalent

____   9. use of cantus firmus structures

____   10. rise of opera and cantata

____   11. chanson and madrigal as major secular forms

____   12. establishment of major/minor tonality

____   13. rise of public theaters

____   14. sonata and concerto as important instrumental forms

____   15. dance music derived from vocal works

*Listen to Gabrieli's motet *O quam suavis* while following the Listening Guide, then answer questions 16–21.

16. What innovations in instrumental music are credited to Giovanni Gabrieli?

_____

_____

_____

17. How does Gabrieli achieve dynamic contrasts in the motet *O quam suavis?*

_____

_____

_____

18. What musical forces (voices and instruments) were used to perform *O quam suavis?*

_____

_____

19. Is the text clearly heard in this work? _____

Explain your answer. _____

20. Do you hear the shifts from duple to triple meter? _____

What musical effect do they have? _____

_____

_____

21. What is the text of *O quam suavis* about? _____

_____

_____

On which religious occasion was it sung? _____

_____

---

24. *Review* **The Organization of Musical Sounds**
Chaps. 17–18

Terms to Remember

key	octave
scale	half step/whole step
chromatic	transposition
diatonic	modulation
major	chords, active and rest
minor	triad
heptatonic	tonic
pentatonic	dominant
tritonic	subdominant
mode	microtone
tonality	raga

Exercises

Complete the following questions.

1. The division of the _____ is variable in musics around the world.

   In Western music, it is divided into _____ equal half steps.

2. How many half steps make up a whole step? _____

3. The distance between C and D is a(n) _____.

4. How many half steps make up the chromatic scale? _____

5. _____ refers to the principle of organization whereby we hear a piece of music in relation to a central tone.

6. The symbol to raise a pitch a half step is a _____ (shown as ____).

7. On the chart below, mark on top the intervals (W for whole step and H for half step) for a major scale, and on the bottom those for a minor scale.

   ```
   major
   scale:   W  _  _  _  _  _  _
          / \ / \ / \ / \ / \ / \ / \
          1   2   3   4   5   6   7   8
          do  re  mi  fa  sol la  ti  do
   minor  \ / \ / \ / \ / \ / \ / \ /
   scale:   _  _  _  _  _  _  _
   ```

8. _____ refers to music built on the seven tones of a major or

   minor scale.

9. _____ refers to music built on all the half steps in the octave.

10. _____ refers to a three-note scale, commonly used in musics of _____ (continent).

11. A five-note scale is referred to as _____ and is commonly heard in musics of _____ (cultures).

12. What is a microtone? _____

_____

13. How do Western listeners typically react to microtones?

_____

14. How is a raga different from a scale? _____

_____

Where are ragas used? _____

15. A three-note chord built on alternating scale tones is called a(n)

_____. When built on the first scale tone, it is called a(n)

_____ chord; when built on the fourth scale tone, it is

called a _____ chord; and when built on the fifth scale

tone, it is called a(n) _____ chord.

16. The shifting of all the tones of a melody by a uniform distance is called

_____.

17. _____ refers to the passing from one key center to another within a composition.

iMusic Listening (Student Resource Disc)

Pop Goes the Weasel

18. Is this built on a ____ major or ____ minor scale? Is it ____ chromatic or ____ diatonic?

Bach: Contrapunctus I, from *The Art of Fugue* (subject and exposition)

19. Is this work built in ____ major or ____ minor tonality?

My Bonnie Lies over the Ocean

20. Describe how active and rest chords function in this song. When is there a sense of tension, and when is there a feeling of finality?

_____

_____

_____

---

25. *Review* **The Baroque and the Arts**
Chaps. 19–20

Exercises

Briefly characterize each of the following in the Baroque.

1. Scientific activity: _____

_____

   Name a scientist from this era. _____

2. Focus of political power: _____

_____

   Name a head of state from this era. _____

3. Religious environment: _____

_____

   What regions of Europe were Protestant? _____

_____

4. Style of painting: _____

_____

   Name an artist from this era. _____

Multiple Choice

_____ 5. The origin of the term "Baroque" is probably:
   a. German, referring to something broken.
   b. Portuguese, referring to an irregularly shaped pearl.
   c. French, referring to a barge-type boat.

_____ 6. The university-based music ensemble that arose in the Baroque
   era is the:
   a. concert band.
   b. collegium musicum.
   c. madrigal choir.

Complete the following questions.

7. Opera had its origins in the experiments of a group known as the

   _____.

8. The new style of music, or *le nuove musiche*, which features solo singing

   with instrumental accompaniment, is called _____.

9. The new accompaniment style was performed on a group of _____ instruments whose players read from a shorthand notation known as _____.

10. The belief that words and music were closely linked is reflected in the _____.

11. The rise of opera was responsible for the popularity of the voice of the _____, a male singer whose high register was preserved through an operation at an early age.

12. The tuning system developed during the Baroque that increased the range of harmonic possibilities was _____.

13. Name several musical devices used for emotional expression in Baroque music. _____

14. What was the significance of the establishment of major/minor tonality in the Baroque? _____
_____
_____

15. What role did improvisation play in Baroque music? Who was expected to improvise? _____
_____
_____

16. What circumstances brought about an increased virtuosity in music?
_____
_____
_____

17. Name several prominent women performers of Baroque music.
_____
_____

> **26.** *Explore* **Music and the Religious Spirit in the New World**
> **CP** 6

Exercises

Complete the following questions.

1. In the seventeenth century, what religion was predominant along the
   eastern seaboard of the United States? _____
   In northeastern Canada? _____ In Mexico? _____

2. Who brought European music to the Amerindians in Mexico?

   _____

3. What type of song is a villancico? _____
   Where was it sung? _____

*4. Who was Juan Gutíerrez de Padilla? _____

   _____

5. What was the basis for much of the early protestant music in the
   Americas? _____

6. Describe the singing style known as "lining out."

   _____

   _____

7. When several embellished versions of the same melody occur
   simultaneously, we call this texture _____.

*8. Name an important eighteenth-century American music teacher and
   composer. _____

*9. What is a fuging tune? _____

   _____

10. What types of devotional music were sung in the nineteenth century?

    _____

    _____

    Was this music of African Americans, whites, or both?

    _____

11. Describe gospel music. _____

_____

_____

12. What is contemporary Christian music? _____

_____

iMusic Listening Assignment (Student Resource Disc)

Listen to the following songs that were popular for worship in the Americas, and read about these two hymns online. Describe the style (music and text) of each and how they enhanced religious or devotional services.

Simple Gifts and *Amazing Grace*

Or visit StudySpace (www.wwnorton.com/enjoy), read this Cultural Perspective, and follow links provided there. Write an essay describing your online research.

_____

_____

_____

_____

_____

_____

_____

_____

_____

_____

_____

_____

_____

_____

_____

_____

_____

_____

_____

_____

---

27. *Review* **Baroque Vocal Forms**
Chaps. 21–24

Exercises

Fill in the answers below.

1. The text of an opera is called the _____ and is written
   by a(n) _____.

2. Operas frequently open with an instrumental introduction called a(n)
   _____.

3. Opera soloists are generally featured in two types of works: a lyrical song
   that allows for emotional expression, called a(n) _____,
   and a disjunct song whose rhythm is fitted to the inflection of the text,
   called a(n) _____.

4. The term "secco" means _____, and the term
   "accompagnato" means _____. Both refer to
   types of _____.

5. An operatic song in the form **A-B-A**, which allows the soloist to embellish
   the last section, is called a(n) _____.

6. The most important early Italian composer of operas was
   _____. His first opera was
   _____.

7. The Italian _____ was a vocal genre for solo singers and
   instrumental accompaniment, set to lyric, dramatic, or narrative poetry.

8. The master of the Baroque oratorio in England was _____.
   His most famous oratorio is _____. Name an opera by
   this same composer. _____

True or False

____ 9. *Tragédie lyrique* was a French opera style associated with Lully.

____ 10. An oratorio is a secular stage work, with sets, costumes, and
        dramatic action.

____ 11. The earliest opera plots were drawn from mythology.

_____ 12. The cantata developed into a multimovement work that features solo vocalists, chorus, and orchestra.

_____ 13. The cantata was central to the service of the Roman Catholic Church.

_____ 14. The masque was a forerunner of the cantata in England.

_____ 15. Many of Bach's cantatas are based on Protestant chorale or hymn tunes.

_____ 16. The oratorio features arias, recitatives, and choruses among its sections.

_____ 17. Cantatas may be either secular or sacred.

_____ 18. Opera seria was Italian comic opera.

_____ 19. Women were not allowed to sing in opera productions.

_____ 20. Barbara Strozzi was a renowned early Baroque composer and singer.

21. What differentiates an opera from an oratorio?

_____

_____

_____

_____

_____

22. What differentiates a cantata from an oratorio?

_____

_____

_____

_____

_____

23. What is the unifying device found in most Lutheran cantatas?

_____

_____

---

28. *Listen* Baroque Opera and the Italian Cantata
*Monteverdi: *The Coronation of Poppea*, excerpt (**LG** 16, *e***LG**)
  Purcell: *Dido and Aeneas*, Dido's Lament and *Chorus (**LG** 17, **Sh** 11, *e***LG**)
*Handel: *Molto voglio*, from *Rinaldo* (**LG** 18, *e***LG**)
  Strozzi: *Begli occhi* (**LG** 19, **Sh** 12, *e***LG**)

Exercises

*Listen to the Monteverdi opera excerpt while following the Listening Guide, then answer questions 1–10.

1. What is the basis for the libretto of *The Coronation of Poppea?*

_____

2. How does the composer portray real human emotions through music?

_____

_____

3. Describe the singing style of the chorus during the coronation.

_____

_____

4. What is the form of the final aria duet? _____

5. What is its structural basis? _____

   Can you hear this throughout? _____

6. What is the "affection" delivered by this aria? _____

7. How does the composer use dissonance for expression?

_____

8. From which period of Monteverdi's life does this opera originate?

_____

9. What was Monteverdi's first opera? _____

10. What was the basis for its plot? _____

Listen to the final scene from the Purcell opera *Dido and Aeneas* while following the Listening Guide, then answer questions 11–16.

11. Where was Purcell teaching when he wrote *Dido and Aeneas?*

_____

12. What is the basis of the libretto for *Dido and Aeneas?* _____

_____

55

13. Describe the style of the recitative "Thy hand, Belinda."

_____

_____

14. What is the structural basis for Dido's aria? _____

_____

Can you hear this throughout?_____

15. How does Purcell use chromaticism as an expressive device?

_____

16. The aria is in two main sections (binary). What is the text where the second section begins?_____

*Listen to the aria *Molto voglio* from Handel's opera *Rinaldo* while following the Listening Guide, then answer questions 17–19.

17. What is the historical setting for this opera?_____

18. Which character sings this aria and why? _____

_____

19. Identify and describe the structure of the aria (both vocal and instrumental parts).

_____

_____

Listen to the Strozzi cantata *Begli occhi* while following the Listening Guide, then answer questions 20–23.

20. What are the performing forces (instruments and/or voices) for Strozzi's cantata *Begli occhi?*

_____

21. How would you characterize the tempo and rhythmic movement in

Begli occhi? _____

22. What specific musical techniques does Strozzi employ to depict the text? _____

_____

23. Describe the role Barbara Strozzi played in the intellectual academies of Venice and the impact she had on the musical genres in which she composed. _____

_____

_____

---

29. *Listen* Bach and the Lutheran Cantata
Bach: Cantata No. 80, *A Mighty Fortress Is Our God*, excerpts (**LG** 20, Sh 13, *eLG*)

Exercises

Listen to the Bach cantata excerpts while following the Listening Guide, read about it, and then answer questions 1–13.

1. What is a chorale tune? _____

2. In a multi-voiced setting, in which voice is the chorale tune generally heard? _____

3. Who wrote the chorale text *Ein feste Burg ist unser Gott?*

   _____

4. How many movements do Bach's cantatas usually have? _____

5. How many movements does Cantata No. 80 have? _____

6. In how many movements does Bach use the chorale tune? _____
   Which movements? _____

7. What is the structure of the first movement of this cantata?

   _____

   Can you easily hear the chorale tune in this setting? _____

*8. What is the structure of the second movement, and where is the chorale tune heard? _____

   _____

*9. What is the "affection" or emotion communicated by this movement (consider its text as well as its music)? _____

*10. Compare the use of the chorale in the first and fifth movements. In which movement is it more prominently heard? _____

   _____

   _____

11. How do the trumpets and timpani contribute to the work? When were these parts added? _____

   _____

   _____

12. What is the primary texture heard in the last movement? _____

13. In which voice part is the chorale tune heard in the last movement?

_____ Can you hear it clearly? _____

14. What was the religious occasion for this cantata?

_____

15. Were you familiar with the chorale tune *A Mighty Fortress Is Our God*

before you heard this work? _____

If yes, where did you learn it? _____

ABOUT THE COMPOSER

16. What were Bach's three important employment positions, and what
kind of music did he write in each?

1st: _____

_____

2nd: _____

_____

3rd: _____

_____

17. What is Bach's most important collection of keyboard works?

_____

18. In which sacred genres did he compose? _____

_____

19. In which instrumental genres did he compose? _____

_____

20. What accounts, in your opinion, for Bach's continued popularity today?

_____

_____

_____

---

30. *Listen* Handel and the Oratorio
Handel: *Messiah*, excerpts (**LG** 21, Sh 14, *e***LG**)

Exercises

Listen to the selections from *Messiah* while following the Listening Guide,
then answer questions 1–10.

1. In which city was *Messiah* premiered? _____

2. What is the source of its text? _____

3. What are the subjects of the three principal sections of the oratorio?

   Part I: _____

   Part II: _____

   Part III: _____

4. What performing forces are required to perform *Messiah*?

   Instrumental: _____

   Vocal: _____

5. The first movement of *Messiah* is an orchestral introduction known as

   a(n) _____.

   *What is its structure? _____

   _____

*6. Describe the difference between the two recitative styles of No. 14.

   _____

   _____

   _____

7. What is the structure of a da capo aria?_____

   Describe how the aria "Rejoice greatly" fits this structure.

   _____

   _____

   _____

8. Listen to the opening of the "Hallelujah Chorus" (iMusic) and describe how Handel changes the texture to create contrast.

_____

_____

_____

9. Cite several examples of word or text painting in this oratorio (any movement). _____

_____

_____

10. What do you think accounts for the continued popularity of this oratorio?

_____

_____

_____

_____

ABOUT THE COMPOSER

11. Where was Handel born? _____

12. What styles of opera did he write? _____

13. Where did he spend most of his career?_____

14. What London musical event changed the public's taste in opera?

_____

15. How did Handel respond to this change in taste?

_____

16. Name several biblical stories on which Handel based oratorios.

_____

17. What ailment did Handel and Bach both suffer late in life?

_____

31. *Review* Baroque Instrumental Forms
Chaps. 25–27

Exercises

Match the correct definitions with the following instrumental forms.

____ 1. solo concerto

a. an organ work in which a traditional chorale tune is embellished

____ 2. concerto grosso

b. a short, continuous piece that often serves to introduce another movement

____ 3. fugue

c. an orchestral introduction, in two repeated sections: slow and fast

____ 4. prelude

d. a multimovement form based on the opposition of one player against a larger group

____ 5. suite

e. a form based on the opposition of a small and a large group

____ 6. trio sonata

f. a series of dance movements, usually in the same key

____ 7. chorale prelude

g. a multimovement work for two violins or other melody instruments and basso continuo

____ 8. French overture

h. an orchestral introduction, in three sections: fast–slow–fast

____ 9. Italian overture

i. a highly structured contrapuntal form, based on a single theme or subject

True or False

____ 10. Vivaldi's *The Four Seasons* comprises four concertos, each based on a poem describing a season.

____ 11. Vivaldi is known principally for his vocal music.

____ 12. The Baroque concerto is most often based on an orchestral refrain, or ritornello procedure.

____ 13. The standard Baroque concerto has three movements.

____ 14. A church sonata (*sonata da chiesa*) is a dance suite for full orchestra.

____ 15. A suite is made up of dance movements, many of which are in binary form.

____ 16. The piano was the most popular Baroque keyboard instrument.

_____ 17. The Italian composer Arcangelo Corelli established the trio sonata structure.

Multiple Choice

_____ 18. Which is NOT a standard dance in the Baroque suite?
   a. gigue
   b. minuet
   c. allemande

_____ 19. Binary form is best outlined as:
   a. **A-B**.
   b. **A-B-A**.
   c. **A-B-C**.

_____ 20. The main theme of a fugue is known as the:
   a. episode.
   b. subject.
   c. fugato.

_____ 21. The answer in a fugue is:
   a. the main theme imitated at another pitch level.
   b. the opening section.
   c. overlapping entries of the main theme.

_____ 22. A section of a fugue in which the main theme is NOT heard is called a(n):
   a. exposition.
   b. episode.
   c. recapitulation.

_____ 23. Which texture best defines a fugue?
   a. homophonic
   b. heterophonic
   c. polyphonic

iMusic Listening (Student Resource Disc)

Minuet in D minor (*Anna Magdalena Notebook*)

24. What is the musical form of this short keyboard work?_____

Bach: *Brandenburg Concerto* No. 1, I

25. Which type of Baroque concerto does this represent? _____ solo concerto or _____ concerto grosso

Handel: Alla hornpipe, from *Water Music*

26. This English dance, from Handel's *Water Music* suite, is set in _____ duple, _____ triple, or _____ quadruple meter.

---

32. *Listen* The Baroque Sonata and Concerto

*Corelli: Trio Sonata, Op. 3, No. 2, Third and Fourth Movements (**LG** 22, *e***LG**)
Vivaldi: *Spring,* from *The Four Seasons* (**LG** 24, Sh 15, *e***LG**)
*Bach: *Brandenburg Concerto* No. 2 in F major, First Movement (**LG** 25, *e***LG**)

Exercises

*Listen to the Corelli Trio Sonata while following the Listening Guide, then answer questions 1–5.

1. The favored trio sonata combination in the Baroque was _____

   and continuo.

2. How many movements does Corelli's Trio Sonata, Op. 3, No. 2, have? ____

3. What is the tempo scheme of the movements? _____

4. What dance type does the third movement resemble? _____

   Describe its musical character. _____

   _____

5. What dance type does the fourth movement resemble? _____

   Describe its musical character. _____

   _____

Listen to the concerto *Spring* by Vivaldi while following the Listening Guide, then answer questions 6–15.

6. What are the two main types of concerto in the Baroque?

   _____

7. Which type is Vivaldi's *Spring?* _____

8. What is the order of movements (by tempo) in this concerto?

   _____

9. What extramusical material determines the form of the work?

   _____

10. What is a ritornello? _____

    _____

11. How many ritornellos are heard in the first movement? _____

12. How many solo episodes are heard? _____

63

13. Do you think Vivaldi was successful in portraying images of springtime?

_____ Explain your answer. _____

_____

14. What elements make this concerto virtuosic? _____

_____

15. Who were the performers that Vivaldi taught and for whom he wrote

much of his instrumental music? _____

_____

*Listen to the first and second movements of Bach's *Brandenburg Concerto*
No. 2 while following the Listening Guide, then answer questions 16–26.

16. What type of concerto is this? _____

17. What is the concerto's overall structure? _____

_____

18. What is the full orchestra called? _____

19. What is the solo group called? _____

20. What instruments make up the solo group in this work?

_____

21. What gives the first movement its forward-moving energy?

_____

_____

22. How many ritornellos are heard in this movement? _____

How do they unify the work? _____

_____

23. How does Bach create contrast in this work? _____

_____

_____

24. Which solo instrument is omitted in the second movement? _____

25. How does the composer make this movement sound emotional?

_____

26. What is the history of the *Brandenburg Concertos?*

_____

_____

> **33.** *Listen* **The Baroque Suite**
> Handel: *Water Music*, Suite in D major, *Allegro and Alla hornpipe (**LG** 26,
> Sh16, *e***LG**)
> Mouret: Rondeau, from *Suite de symphonies* (**LG** 27, Sh17, *e***LG**)

Exercises

Fill in the answers below.

1. The Baroque suite comprised a number of dances in the same key. List the
   four standard ones below, with country of origin and musical character.

   Dance _____ Country _____

   Character _____

   Dance _____ Country _____

   Character _____

   Dance _____ Country _____

   Character _____

   Dance _____ Country _____

   Character _____

2. List some dances that are frequently added to a suite.

   _____

3. Which Baroque composer wrote the suite entitled *Tafelmusik?*

   _____ What does this title mean? _____

   _____

Listen to the *Allegro and Alla hornpipe from Handel's *Water Music* while
following the Listening Guide, then answer questions 4–14.

*4. What is the form of the Allegro from the *Water Music* suite?

   _____

*5. What instruments are featured in the fanfare opening?

   _____

6. Where was the *Water Music* suite first performed?

   _____

7. What instruments were lacking in this performance?

   _____

8. What is another well-known orchestral suite by Handel?

_____

9. What instruments are first heard in the Alla hornpipe?

_____

10. What other instruments are featured during the movement?

_____

11. What is the form of the Alla hornpipe? _____

12. In the **B** section, the harmony shifts from D major to B minor. Can you hear the difference? _____

13. What instruments are heard in the **B** section? _____

_____

14. Describe the timbre of some of the Baroque period instruments in this recording, noting how they differ from their modern counterparts.

_____

_____

_____

_____

_____

_____

Listen to the Rondeau by the French composer Mouret while following the Listening Guide, then answer questions 15–18.

15. What is the overall form of the rondeau?

_____ binary _____ ternary _____ 5-part sectional

16. How would you describe the character of the opening of this work?

_____

17. What television program uses this work as its theme song?

_____

18. What is a divertissement? _____

---

34. *Listen* **Baroque Keyboard Music**
*Scarlatti: Sonata in C major, K. 159 (*The Hunt*) (**LG** 23, **eLG**)
  Bach: Contrapunctus 1, from *The Art of Fugue* (**LG** 28, Sh 18, **eLG**)

Exercises

*Listen to the Scarlatti Sonata in C major, K. 159, and answer questions 1–7 below.

1. What did Scarlatti call his keyboard sonatas? _____

2. Approximately how many did he write? _____ For what instrument?

   _____

3. How many movements are typical in a Scarlatti sonata? _____

4. What gives our sonata, K. 159, the nickname of "The Hunt"?

   _____

5. The composer calls for short, ornamental notes played before the beat.

   These are called _____.

6. Describe the form of the Sonata in C major, K. 159. _____

   _____

7. How does the composer evoke Spanish effects in this sonata?

   _____

   _____

Listen to Contrapunctus I from *The Art of Fugue* and answer questions 8–10 below.

8. Bach's monumental collection *The Art of Fugue* includes _____ fugues

   and _____ canons.

9. What is the main theme of the fugue called? _____

   What is it called when the same theme is stated on the dominant?

   _____

10. How many statements of the main theme are heard in the exposition

   of this fugue? _____ Can you hear them easily played on the organ?

   _____

iMusic Listening (Student Resource Disc)

Bach: Contrapunctus I, from *The Art of Fugue,* exposition

Listen to the version of the exposition played by modern brass instruments.

11. Are the entries of the theme easier to hear in this performance?_____

12. What term best describes the overall texture of this fugue?

   _____

13. What term is used for sections of a fugue in which the main theme is

   not heard? _____

Listen to the various permutations of the theme and describe each:

14. augmentation: _____

15. diminution: _____

16. inversion: _____

17. retrograde: _____

True/False

____ 18. Bach probably wrote *The Art of Fugue* for the piano.

____ 19. This fugue is set in a minor key.

____ 20. This fugue ends in the key in which it began.

____ 21. Bach wrote only instrumental fugues.

____ 22. The term "fugue" derives from the word for "the hunt."

____ 23. Bach's *Well-Tempered Clavier* is a collection of 48 preludes and
     fugues.

____ 24. A fugue is usually based on two distinct themes.

25. Based on the quote by J. S. Bach's son in your text, what was the
    importance of *The Art of Fugue?*

   _____

   _____

   _____

---

35. *Review* From Baroque to Classical
Trans. II

Exercises

Complete the following questions.

1. What does the word "Rococo" mean? _____

2. What are the major characteristics of Rococo art? _____

   _____

   Name a well-known painter of the era. _____

3. Name two French composers that represent this style.

   _____

4. What traits were composers breaking away from in the Rococo?

   _____

   _____

5. What were the goals of the new "sensitive" style?

   _____

6. What major instrumental genres were developed during this era?

   _____

7. What was important about the premiere of *The Beggar's Opera?*

   _____

   _____

8. What brought on the "War of the Buffoons"?

   _____

   _____

9. What changes did Gluck wish to bring about in opera seria?

   _____

   _____

10. What subjects did Gluck explore in his operas? _____

    _____

For each of the traits listed below, indicate with the appropriate letter the style to which it best relates.

      a. Baroque style
      b. Classical style

____ 11. polyphonic textures

____ 12. single "affection" for each work or movement

____ 13. symmetrical and balanced phrases

____ 14. forte/piano contrasts and echo effects

____ 15. improvisation limited to cadenzas

____ 16. symphony and string quartet prevalent

____ 17. organ and harpsichord as solo instruments

____ 18. use of chromatic harmony for expression

____ 19. piano as favored solo instrument

____ 20. use of clarinet in orchestra

____ 21. use of crescendos and decrescendos

22. Name the major composers of the Baroque era.

_____

Which of these did you know of prior to this course?

_____

23. Name the major composers of the Classical era.

_____

Which of these did you know of prior to this course?

_____

---

36. *Review* Expanded Elements of Form
Chaps. 28–29

Exercises

Fill in the answers below.

1. The smallest unit of a melody is called a(n) _____.

2. The principal melody in a composition is called a(n) _____.

3. The manipulation and expansion of this melody is known as

_____.

4. Name several techniques through which musical material is developed.

_____

Multiple Choice

_____ 5. How many movements are found in the typical multimovement
cycle?
a. one   c. four
b. two   d. six

_____ 6. Which of the following genres is often in a multimovement cycle
form?
a. string quartet   c. sonata
b. symphony   d. all of the above

_____ 7. Which of the following is the standard form for the first movement
in a multimovement cycle?
a. theme and variations form c. minuet and trio form
b. sonata-allegro form   d. binary (**A-B**) form

_____ 8. Which are the three main sections of this first-movement form?
a. exposition–development–coda
b. exposition–development–recapitulation
c. minuet–trio–minuet
d. theme–variation 1–variation 2

_____ 9. The section of a form that serves as a transition, often to another
key center, is known as a:
a. codetta.   c. bridge.
b. theme group.   d. development.

_____ 10. The final section of a movement that rounds off the piece,
re-establishing the tonic key, is called the:
a. bridge.   c. introduction.
b. development.   d. coda.

_____ 11. What is the standard tempo scheme of a multimovement cycle?
      a. fast–moderate–slow–fast   c. fast–slow–moderate–fast
      b. slow–fast–moderate–fast   d. fast–slow–fast–slow

12. Describe how the two principal themes of a sonata-allegro form differ from each other.

    Theme (or theme group) 1   Theme (or theme group) 2

    _____

    _____

13. How does the final section or restatement of earlier themes differ from what is heard in the exposition?

    _____

14. What is the purpose of the development section?

    _____

    _____

15. What elements can be varied in a theme and variations form?

    _____

    _____

True or False

_____ 16. Minuet and trio form is most often found as the fourth movement of a sonata cycle.

_____ 17. A minuet and trio is generally in duple meter.

_____ 18. A rondo features one main idea that keeps coming back throughout the work.

_____ 19. A coda provides an introduction to a movement.

_____ 20. Form is an important element in absolute music.

iMusic Listening (Student Resource Disc)

Beethoven: Symphony No 5, I

21. Describe some of the ways Beethoven develops musical ideas in this short excerpt from his Symphony No. 5.

    _____

    _____

    _____

    _____

37. *Review* The Classical Spirit
Chaps. 30–31

Exercises

Fill in the answers below.

1. List general attributes of the Classical style that parallel those listed for the Romantic.

Classical

a. _____

   _____

b. _____

c. _____

   _____

d. _____

Romantic

a. longing for strangeness, ecstasy, and wonder

b. intense subjectivity

c. symbolized by Dionysus, God of passion and intoxication

d. uninhibited emotional expression

Choose the best answer for each.

_____ 2. Which historical event took place first?
    a. French Revolution
    b. American Revolution

_____ 3. Which culture was idealized in the eighteenth century?
    a. the medieval world
    b. the world of ancient Greece and Rome

_____ 4. Which eighteenth-century movement helped shape the modern world?
    a. the Protestant Reformation
    b. the Industrial Revolution

Match the following Classical-era figures with their correct descriptions.

_____ 5. Friedrich von Schiller

_____ 6. Thomas Jefferson

_____ 7. Jacques Louis David

_____ 8. Catherine the Great

_____ 9. Eli Whitney

a. French revolutionary painter

b. enlightened czarina of Russia

c. principal author of the Declaration of Independence

d. English experimenter who invented the cotton gin

e. German early Romantic poet

73

10. Who are the four musical masters of the Viennese school?

   a. _____   c. _____

   b. _____   d. _____

11. Check those characteristics below that properly describe the Classical musical style (one check per grouping).

_____ a. disjunct, wide-ranging melodies *or*
_____ b. simple, singable melodies

_____ c. regular, symmetrical phrasing with clear cadences *or*
_____ d. irregular, asymmetrical phrasing with weak or covered cadences

_____ e. chromatic harmony *or*
_____ f. diatonic harmony

_____ g. free, programmatic forms *or*
_____ h. large-scale, absolute forms

_____ i. incorporation of folk songs and dances *or*
_____ j. incorporation of non-Western melodies

_____ k. weak or free meters *or*
_____ l. strong, regular meters

12. How would you describe the patronage system? What were the advantages and disadvantages to artists serving under this system?

_____

_____

_____

_____

_____

13. What role did women play in music during this era?

_____

_____

_____

_____

38. *Explore* The "Mozart Effect"
CP 7

Exercises

Complete the following questions.

1. What kind of brain changes seem to take place in a listener who has just heard Mozart's Sonata for Two Pianos, K. 448?

_____

_____

_____

2. Review the chart in your text of how the brain interprets the opening of this sonata. Comment on the symmetry in the graph.

_____

_____

_____

3. Who is the physicist associated with this research? _____

4. Besides listening to classical music, what are some other activities that require high-level brain functions involving spatial-temporal reasoning?

_____

5. How does this research promise to help people with disorders such as autism or epilepsy?

_____

_____

_____

6. Do you think the phenomenon is connected with Mozart's talents as a child prodigy? _____ Why or why not? _____

7. Have you ever experienced a sense of enhanced reasoning skills?

_____ During or after what activity? _____

_____

Essay

Locate a recording of a Mozart piano sonata in your campus library or purchase one from iTunes. Listen to it, focusing on the motivic structure and repetition patterns. Refrain from other activities while listening, and stay focused on the music for ten to fifteen minutes. Then try a tough math or logic problem. Do you notice any enhanced ability? Comment below.

Or visit StudySpace (www.wwnorton.com/enjoy), read this Cultural Perspective, and follow links provided there. Write an essay describing your online research.

---

39. *Review* **Chamber Music and Symphony in the Classical Era**
Chaps. 32–34

Exercises

CHAMBER MUSIC

Answer the following questions.

1. What is chamber music? _____

2. What was the favored chamber ensemble in the Classical era, and what

   are its components? _____

   _____

3. Name several other common chamber ensembles. _____

   _____

4. Name several forms of popular-entertainment music during the

   Classical era. _____

Match each of the following string quartet movements with the form it
would most likely take.

_____ 5. first movement   a. theme and variations form

_____ 6. second movement   b. rondo form

_____ 7. third movement   c. sonata-allegro form

_____ 8. fourth movement   d. minuet and trio form

Match each of the following string quartet traits with the composer best
associated with it.

_____ 9. use of folk elements   a. Mozart

_____ 10. scherzo replacing minuet   b. Haydn

_____ 11. motivic development   c. Beethoven

_____ 12. lyrical, elegant themes

THE SYMPHONY

13. Out of which earlier form did the symphony evolve? _____

14. What contributions did Mannheim musicians make to the symphony?

    _____

15. Approximately how many players made up a Classical-era orchestra? _____ Which instrument families are represented? _____

    _____

16. In what type of setting were symphonies performed in the eighteenth century? _____

    In what setting are they performed today? _____

17. Which movement of the symphony is generally the longest and the most complex? _____

    What is its form? _____

18. Which movement is generally the fastest? _____

    What are typical forms for this movement? _____

    _____

19. Which movement is based on a dance form? _____

    What is the character of this dance movement? _____

    _____

20. Which movement is generally the slowest? _____

    What forms are typical for it? _____

    _____

21. Which movement is probably the most lyrical? _____

22. What does the term "monothematic" mean relating to the symphony?

    _____

    Which composer is associated with this form?

    _____

---

40. *Listen* Eighteenth-Century Chamber Music
*Haydn: String Quartet Op. 76, No. 2, Fourth Movement (**LG** 30, *e***LG**)
Mozart: *Eine kleine Nachtmusik*, K. 525 (**LG** 31, Sh 19, *e***LG**)

Exercises

*Listen to the last movement of Haydn's String Quartet Op. 76, No. 2, while following the Listening Guide, then answer questions 1–8.

1. How many string quartets did Haydn write? _____

2. When were his Opus 76 quartets written? _____

3. In which key is Op. 76, No. 2 written? _____

4. How many movements does this quartet have? _____

5. Give the general tempo and form for each movement.

    I. _____

    II. _____

    III. _____

    IV. _____

6. What is the nickname for this quartet? _____

    Why is it called this? _____

7. What elements make the fourth movement sound dance-like?

    _____

    _____

8. Describe the sound of the Classical-period string instruments on this

    recording. _____

    _____

Listen to Mozart's *Eine kleine Nachtmusik* while following the Listening Guide, then answer questions 9–20.

9. What does the title *Eine kleine Nachtmusik* mean literally?

    _____

10. Is this work _____ a string quartet or _____ a serenade?

    What size ensemble was it written for? _____

11. List the general tempo and form for each movement.

I. _____

II. _____

III. _____

IV. _____

iMusic Listening (Student Resource Disc)

Mozart: *Eine kleine Nachtmusik,* I

12. How would you describe the themes heard in this movement?

First theme: _____

Second theme: _____

13. What are some ways Mozart achieves contrast in this movement?

_____

_____

_____

Mozart: *Eine kleine Nachtmusik,* III

14. How would you describe the opening minuet theme?

_____

15. Can you hear the short, repeated sections? _____

16. Are the phrases balanced and regular in length? _____

17. Describe the trio theme and how it contrasts with the minuet.

_____

_____

18. Which section sounds more like a dance? Why? _____

_____

19. For what kind of concert setting was this piece written? _____

_____

_____

20. Do you think people danced to the minuet? _____

---

41. *Listen* The Eighteenth-Century Symphony
*Mozart: Symphony No. 40, First Movement (**LG** 32, *e***LG**)
 Haydn: Symphony No. 94, Second Movement (**LG** 33. Sh 20, *e***LG**)
 Beethoven: Symphony No. 5 (**LG** 34, Sh 21, *e***LG**)

Exercises

*Listen to Mozart's Symphony No. 40 in G minor while following the
Listening Guide, then answer questions 1–4.

1. What is the overall form of this symphony (movements and tempo)?

   _____

   _____

2. Describe the motive that provides the building block for the first theme.

   _____

3. Unlike many Classical-era symphonies, Mozart's Symphony No. 40 is in
   the minor mode. What effect is produced by this choice of harmony?

   _____

   _____

4. Why was this symphony called the "Romantic" by the Viennese?

   _____

   _____

iMusic Listening (Student Resource Disc)

Mozart: Symphony No. 40, III

5. Listen to the minuet and trio from this same symphony and comment
   on the mood set by the minor key and dramatic character.

   _____

   _____

Listen to Haydn's Symphony No. 94, second movement, and Beethoven's
Symphony No. 5 while following the Listening Guides, then answer
questions 6–12.

6. Complete the following chart.

	SYMPHONY NO. 94	SYMPHONY NO. 5
a. First movement		
Tempo:	_____	_____
Form:	_____	_____

81

b. Second movement

Tempo: _____   _____

Form: _____   _____

c. Third movement

Tempo: _____   _____

Form: _____   _____

d. Fourth movement

Tempo: _____   _____

Form: _____   _____

7. Do both symphonies follow the standard multimovement cycle plan?

_____

8. How does Haydn "surprise" his listeners in the second movement of Symphony No. 94? _____

_____

9. What are the differences in size and instrumentation between Haydn's orchestra and Beethoven's? _____

_____

10. What makes the first movement of Beethoven's Symphony No. 5 so memorable? _____

_____

11. What traits of the Beethoven symphony sound Romantic?

_____

_____

12. What are some of the innovations that Beethoven introduced in this symphony? _____

_____

_____

_____

---

42. *Review* The Classical Masters
Chaps. 33, 35–36

Exercises

For each of the following, choose the composer who best fits the description.

    a. Joseph Haydn
    b. Wolfgang Amadeus Mozart
    c. Ludwig van Beethoven

_____ 1. The composer who was a child prodigy as a composer and performer.

_____ 2. The composer who grew deaf at the height of his compositional career.

_____ 3. The composer generally known as the "father of the symphony."

_____ 4. The composer who died young, while writing a Requiem Mass.

_____ 5. The composer who thrived for many years under the patronage system.

_____ 6. The composer of the "London" symphonies.

_____ 7. The composer of thirty-two piano sonatas, including the *Moonlight.*

_____ 8. The composer who is well-known for opera buffa.

_____ 9. The composer whose last symphony includes a choral setting of Schiller's *Ode to Joy.*

_____ 10. The composer who spanned the transition between the Classical and Romantic eras.

11. List for comparison the number of symphonies written by each composer below.

    Haydn _____   Mozart _____   Beethoven _____

12. Why did Mozart write fewer symphonies than Haydn?

    _____

    _____

13. Why did Beethoven write fewer symphonies than Haydn or Mozart?

    _____

    _____

14. What European country can be associated with the lives of all three of these musicians? _____

Choose the best answer for each.

____ 15. The K. number following each Mozart work refers to the:
     a. name of the man who catalogued his compositions.
     b. key, or tonality, of the composition.

____ 16. Which Mozart opera was written in German and was popular in the Viennese theater?
     a. *The Magic Flute*
     b. *The Marriage of Figaro*

____ 17. Haydn worked for many years for the:
     a. Prince-Archbishop of Salzburg.
     b. Hungarian noble family of Esterházy.

____ 18. Which was a popular oratorio by Haydn?
     a. *The Creation*
     b. *Messiah*

____ 19. Which composer wrote only one opera, *Fidelio?*
     a. Joseph Haydn
     b. Ludwig van Beethoven

____ 20. Late in his life, Haydn made several visits to _____, where he was commissioned to write a group of symphonies.
     a. Italy
     b. England

____ 21. The composer of the *Eroica* Symphony was:
     a. Beethoven.
     b. Mozart.

22. How do you account for the continued popularity of these three Classical composers?

_____

_____

_____

_____

_____

43. *Explore* Beethoven and the Politics of Music
CP 8

Exercises

Answer the following questions.

1. Who was the famous French general that Beethoven once admired?

   _____

2. What works did he dedicate (or plan to dedicate) to him? _____

   _____

3. Why did Beethoven become disillusioned with this ruler? _____

   _____

   _____

4. For what occasion did Beethoven write his famous *Battle Symphony*?

   _____

*5. What tunes did he incorporate in this work? _____

   _____

*6. For what unusual instrument was this work first conceived?

   _____

7. When is this *Battle Symphony* performed today? _____

   _____

8. On what text did Beethoven base the last movement of his Symphony

   No. 9? _____

9. What inspired him to choose his text? _____

10. What countries and cultures have adopted this inspirational choral

    setting? _____

    _____

Listening Assignment

Locate a recording (or video) of Beethoven's Symphony No. 9. Listen to the finale (the fourth movement), read the text, and describe the work below.

Or visit StudySpace (www.wwnorton.com/enjoy), read this Cultural Perspective, and follow links provided there. Write an essay describing your online research.

What is the text of this movement about? _____

_____

_____

Describe the melody sung by the soloists and chorus.

_____

_____

Describe the march (about eight minutes into the movement). Consider the meter and instruments used.

_____

_____

_____

_____

_____

_____

What other musical elements help to deliver the message of the text?

_____

_____

_____

_____

Why do you think this work has been popular the world over?

_____

_____

_____

_____

44. *Review* The Concerto and Sonata in the Classical Era
Chaps. 37–38

Exercises

Multiple Choice

____ 1. How many movements are standard in a concerto?
    a. two   c. four
    b. three   d. five or more

____ 2. How many movements are standard in a sonata?
    a. one or two   c. three or four
    b. two or three   d. five or more

____ 3. Which tempo scheme is standard for the concerto?
    a. slow–fast   c. fast–slow–fast
    b. fast–slow–fast–faster   d. slow–moderate–fast

4. What is a cadenza, and when is it usually played? _____

_____

_____

5. What two forms does the first movement of a concerto adapt?

_____

6. What were the solo instruments favored in the Classical concerto?

_____

7. What instrument(s) did Mozart play?

_____

8. For whom did he write his Piano Concerto in G major, K. 453?

_____

9. What were the instruments favored in the Classical sonata?

_____

10. What is a duo sonata? _____

_____

Match the following virtuoso performers with their correct descriptions.

a. Barbara von Ployer   c. Maria Anna Mozart
b. Maddalena Lombardini   d. Maria Theresa von Paradis

_____ 11. An accomplished pianist who was Mozart's sister.

_____ 12. A gifted piano student of Mozart's, for whom he wrote two concertos.

_____ 13. A talented blind pianist and organist, for whom both Mozart and Salieri wrote concertos.

_____*14. A virtuoso violinist who was a student of Tartini and also a composer of violin concertos.

iMusic Listening (Student Resource Disc)

Mozart: Clarinet Concerto, II

15. What is the likely tempo marking for this movement? _____

16. Is this typical for the second movement of a concerto? _____

17. Describe the main theme and the mood Mozart sets.

_____

_____

18. Describe how the solo clarinet—a new invention in Mozart's day—interacts with the rest of the orchestra in this excerpt.

_____

_____

_____

45. *Explore* **East Meets West: Turkish Influences on the Viennese Classics**

CP 9

Exercises

Answer the following questions.

1. To which empire did eighteenth-century Austria belong?

   _____

   To which empire did Turkey belong? _____

2. What is a Janissary band? _____

   _____

   When and where did it originate? _____

3. How did Western Europeans come to know the sound of the Janissary

   ensemble? _____

   _____

4. What instruments were added to this band in the seventeenth century?

   _____

   _____

5. Which Classical composers tried to imitate the Janissary band in their

   music? _____

6. What permanent contribution did this ensemble make to the Western

   orchestra? _____

   _____

7. What other Western music group did the Janissary ensemble influence?

   _____

8. Which Islamic religious ceremony did Beethoven attempt to imitate in

   The Ruins of Athens? _____

   Describe this ceremony. _____

   _____

   _____

iMusic Listening Assignment (Student Resource Disc)

Listen to Haydn's *Military* Symphony and describe how you think the composer was influenced by the Turkish Janissary band. Why does the symphony (No. 100) have the subtitle *Military*?

Or visit StudySpace (www.wwnorton.com/enjoy), read this Cultural Perspective, and follow links provided there. Write an essay describing your online research.

---

46. *Listen* The Classical Concerto and Sonata

Mozart: Piano Concerto in G major, K. 453, First Movement; *Second and
*Third Movements (**LG** 35, Sh 22, *e***LG**)
*Haydn: Trumpet Concerto in E-flat major, Third Movement (**LG** 36, *e***LG**)
Beethoven: Piano Sonata in C-sharp minor (*Moonlight*), First, Second, *Third
Movements (**LG** 38, Sh 23, *e***LG**)
*Mozart: Piano Sonata in A major, K. 331, Third Movement (**LG** 37, *e***LG**)

Exercises

Listen to the Mozart piano concerto while following the Listening Guide,
then answer questions 1–6.

1. Describe the characters of the themes as stated by the orchestra in the
   first movement.

   Theme 1: _____

   Theme 2: _____

2. Describe the first theme as heard in the solo exposition with piano.

   _____

   _____

3. How many times and where do you hear the "piano theme"?

   _____

   _____

4. What is a cadenza? _____

   What themes do you recognize in the first-movement cadenza?

   _____

*5. How would you describe the mood of the second movement?

   _____

*6. In the third movement, describe each variation of the theme.

   Variation 1: _____

   Variation 2: _____

   Variation 3: _____

   Variation 4: _____

   Variation 5: _____

*Listen to the third movement of Haydn's Trumpet Concerto while following the Listening Guide, then answer questions 7–8.

7. Describe the instrument for which this concerto was written. How does it differ from the modern trumpet? _____

_____

8. What is the form of the movement? _____

Listen to Beethoven's *Moonlight* Sonata, then answer questions 9–11.

9. How did this piano sonata get the name *Moonlight*?

_____

_____

10. What could be viewed as "Romantic" about the *Moonlight* sonata?

_____

_____

11. What is the form and tempo of each movement?

    I. _____

    II. _____

    III. _____

*Listen to Mozart's Piano Sonata in A major while following the Listening Guide, then answer questions 12–14.

12. What is the form of this movement? _____

What is the meter? _____

13. Why is it subtitled "alla turca"? What are the special effects heard in this movement? _____

_____

_____

14. The Mozart concerto and sonata and the Beethoven sonata feature the piano as a solo instrument. How do you account for the popularity of the piano in the eighteenth century?

_____

_____

_____

_____

---

*47. *Listen* Haydn and Classical Choral Music
*Mozart: *Dies irae*, from Requiem (**LG 39, *eLG***)
*Haydn: *The Creation*, Part I, Nos. 12–14 (**LG 40, *eLG***)

Exercises

Answer the following questions on choral forms.

1. What is the difference between a Mass and a Requiem Mass?

_____

_____

*Listen to the excerpt from Mozart's Requiem while following the Listening Guide, then answer questions 2–4.

2. When did Mozart write his Requiem Mass? Why did he not complete it?

_____

3. What is the *Dies irae* text about? _____

_____

4. Describe some of the ways that Mozart varies his musical treatment of this powerful text.

_____

_____

_____

_____

*Listen to the excerpts from Haydn's *The Creation* while following the Listening Guide, then answer questions 5–13.

5. What were the literary sources for the text of *The Creation?*

_____

_____

6. Which biblical characters are featured in the oratorio?

_____

_____

7. What is memorable about Haydn's treatment of the words "Let there

be light"? _____

_____

8. There are two types of recitative in this excerpt. Describe how each sounds, and give a line of text where each style is heard.

secco: _____

text: _____

accompagnato: _____

text: _____

9. Which day of creation does Uriel's recitative describe? _____

According to the text, what was created on that day? _____

_____

10. How would you describe the texture of the opening of the chorus (on

the text "The Heavens are telling")? _____

11. At which point in the text do you hear the soloists singing in imitation

(overlapping entries)? _____

12. Describe in your own words the mood of this chorus.

_____

_____

_____

13. Would a modern choral work on this text and subject be effective

today? _____ Why or why not? _____

_____

_____

_____

48. *Listen* Mozart's *The Marriage of Figaro*

Mozart: *The Marriage of Figaro,* *Overture and Act I, Scenes 6 and 7 (**LG** 41, Sh 24, *e***LG**)

Exercises

Listen to the selections on your recording from *The Marriage of Figaro* while following the Listening Guide, then answer the questions below.

1. What type (genre) of opera is this? _____

2. What are some of the typical characteristics of this opera type?

_____

_____

3. How does this opera type differ from opera seria? _____

_____

_____

4. Who was the librettist for *The Marriage of Figaro?*

_____

5. Name several Mozart operas by the same librettist.

_____

6. What was the literary basis for *The Marriage of Figaro?*

_____

7. In what ways does this opera satirize the aristocracy?

_____

_____

8. What is a trouser role? _____

_____

9. Is the trouser role convincing in *The Marriage of Figaro?* _____

10. What do you learn about the character of Cherubino from the aria

(No. 6)? _____

_____

11. What purpose is served by the long recitative between Cherubino's aria and the trio in *The Marriage of Figaro?*

_____

_____

_____

12. Consider the three characters singing in the trio (No. 7), and suggest below what emotion each is expressing and how the music helps communicate this emotion.

The Count: _____

_____

Basilio: _____

_____

Susanna: _____

_____

13. What aspects of the plot of *The Marriage of Figaro* strike you as unrealistic or far-fetched?

_____

_____

_____

14. How would this story be changed in a modern-day update?

_____

_____

_____

---

49. *Review* **Schubert and the Transition from Classicism to Romanticism**

Trans. III

Exercises

Answer the following questions.

1. Which Classical master's music foreshadowed the Romantic style?

   _____

2. What are some of the Romantic characteristics in his music?

   _____

   _____

3. Which early Romantic composer can be viewed as the direct heir of the Classical tradition? _____

4. In which genres is this composer considered Classical?

   _____

   In which genres is he more Romantic in style? _____

5. What is a Lied? _____

6. What Romantic fascination does the song *The Trout* represent?

   _____

7. What chamber work did Schubert base on his song *The Trout?*

   _____

COMPARING CLASSICAL AND ROMANTIC STYLES

8. Name the three great Classical masters.

   _____

9. Name at least three Romantic composers.

   _____

   _____

For each of the following musical traits, indicate whether it is best associated with the Classical or the Romantic style.

        a. Classical style
        b. Romantic style

____ 10. interest in the bizarre and macabre

____ 11. diatonic harmony predominant

____ 12. use of unusual ranges of instruments

____ 13. use of one-movement programmatic forms

____ 14. dance rhythms with regular beats and accents

____ 15. rise of a middle-class audience

____ 16. use of freer rhythms and tempo rubato

____ 17. emotional restraint

____ 18. symmetrical, balanced phrases

____ 19. wide-ranging dynamic contrasts

____ 20. introduction of the English horn and tuba

____ 21. preference for absolute forms

____ 22. sonata-allegro form established

____ 23. aristocratic audiences

____ 24. much expanded melodic and harmonic chromaticism

25. What are the approximate dates of the Classical period?

_____ the Romantic period? _____

26. Do you think the arts today lean more toward Romantic or Classical traits? _____ Explain your answer.

_____

_____

_____

_____

_____

---

50. *Listen* Schubert: From Song to Chamber Music
*Schubert: *The Trout* and *Trout* Quintet, Fourth Movement (**LG 42**, *e***LG**)

Exercises

*Listen to the two works listed above while following the Listening Guide, then answer the questions below.

1. Who wrote the poem *The Trout?* _____

2. What is the poem's form? _____

3. What is the German title of this poem? _____

4. Describe the story told in the poem. _____

_____

5. What is the musical form of Schubert's song *The Trout?*

_____

6. How and where is the music modified? _____

_____

7. What role does the piano play in telling the story? _____

_____

8. What is folk-like about this song? _____

_____

9. For which movement of his Piano Quintet did Schubert use this song?

_____

10. What is the instrumentation of the Piano Quintet?

_____

11. What is unusual about this instrumentation? _____

_____

12. How many movements does this quintet have? _____

    Is this number typical? _____

13. What is the form of the fourth movement? _____

14. The main theme is heard in two parts, with each repeated. Which part

    is longer? _____

15. For each variation, note which instrument(s) has(have) the main melody.

Variation 1: _____

Variation 2: _____

Variation 3: _____

Variation 4: _____

Variation 5: _____

Variation 6: _____

16. In which variation does the harmony shift to a minor key?

_____

How does this shift affect the mood?

_____

17. Does this quintet seem Classical or Romantic in style? Explain.

_____

_____

_____

51. *Review* The Romantic Movement
Chaps. 41–42, Sh 40–41

Exercises

Answer the following questions.

1. What were the ideals of the early Romantic movement?

_____

_____

2. What social changes resulted from the French Revolution?

_____

_____

3. What was the slogan of the revolution? _____

Match the following Romantic figures with their descriptions on the right.

_____ 4. Heinrich Heine a. English novelist

_____ 5. Victor Hugo b. French painter

_____ 6. Eugène Delacroix c. German poet

_____ 7. Nathaniel Hawthorne d. American writer

_____ 8. Emily Brontë e. French novelist

9. What effect did the Industrial Revolution have on the production of
musical instruments? _____

_____

_____

_____

10. What new instruments were developed in the Romantic era?

_____

_____

_____

11. Which sections of the orchestra grew substantially during the Romantic
era? _____

_____

101

12. How were educational opportunities in music affected during the era?

_____

_____

13. What is meant by "exoticism" in music? _____

_____

_____

14. Name a musical work that represents exoticism.

   Composer: _____ Title: _____

Multiple Choice

_____ 15. Which of the following is NOT typical of Romantic music?
   a. lyrical, singable melodies
   b. expanded forms
   c. smaller orchestras
   d. increased dissonance for expression

_____ 16. Which role did Romantic composers generally NOT fill?
   a. educators
   b. servants to the aristocracy
   c. performing artists
   d. conductors

Complete the following questions.

17. Who were the musical "stars" in the nineteenth century?

_____

_____

18. What roles in music did women fill in the Romantic era?

_____

_____

19. What educational opportunities in music were open to women?

_____

_____

20. What prejudices did women musicians, artists, and writers have to contend with in the nineteenth century?

_____

_____

_____

_____

---

52. *Review* The Nineteenth-Century Art Song
Chaps. 43–46, Sh 42–45

Exercises

Complete the following questions.

1. A song form often heard in popular music in which the same melody is repeated for each stanza is known as _____.

2. A song that is composed from beginning to end without repetitions of whole sections is in a form called _____.

3. A song type that features some repetition or variations of a melody along with new material is known as _____.

4. A group of Lieder unified by a descriptive or narrative theme is known as a(n) _____. Name one and its composer.

_____

True or False

____ 5. A Lied is a German art song for solo voice and piano.

____ 6. Folk elements are sometimes incorporated into the Lied.

____ 7. The composer normally writes the lyrics for the Lied.

____ 8. The Lied composer often attempts to portray the imagery of the poem musically.

____ 9. Favorite themes of the Lied include love and nature.

____ 10. The piano was declining in popularity at the time of the Romantic Lied.

11. Name one important German poet whose texts were frequently set to music; list one specific work and its composer.

POET   WORK   COMPOSER

_____   _____   _____

12. Name two additional important composers of Lieder.

a. _____

b. _____

13. When was Schubert's *Erlking* written? _____

    How old was the composer when he wrote it?_____

    Who wrote the poem? _____

14. What is Schubert's *Winter's Journey?* _____

15. Approximately how many songs did Schubert write? _____

*16. What is a "Schubertiad"? _____

SCHUMANN AS A LIED COMPOSER

*17. About how many songs did Robert Schumann write? _____

18. What is the most common theme in Schumann's songs?

    _____

19. Name two song cycles by Robert Schumann.

    _____

20. To whose texts is Schumann's *A Poet's Love* set? _____

21. What is the theme of this song cycle? Does it tell a story? _____

    _____

    _____

    _____

53. *Listen* Romantic Lieder
Schubert: *Erlking* (**LG** 43, Sh 25, *e***LG**)
Schumann: "In the lovely month of May," from *A Poet's Love* (**LG** 44, Sh 26, *e***LG**)

Exercises

Listen to Schubert's *Erlking* while following the Listening Guide, then answer questions 1–5.

1. How does the piano establish the mood of Schubert's *Erlking* at the

   beginning of the song? _____

   _____

2. What is the form of this song? _____

   Is any music or idea repeated? _____

3. Describe how Schubert portrays each of the four characters in the song musically with only one singer.

   Narrator: _____

   Father: _____

   Son: _____

   Erlking: _____

4. How does Schubert use dissonance for dramatic effect?

   _____

5. Bearing in mind the drama of Schubert's *Erlking*, suggest a story (either from literature or from a movie) that you think would make a successful Lied, with solo voice and piano. Briefly describe the story and suggest some effects that might be achieved in the Lied.

   _____

   _____

   _____

   _____

   _____

   _____

105

Listen to Robert Schumann's "In the lovely month of May," from *A Poet's Love,* while following the Listening Guide, then answer questions 6–10.

6. What is the form of this song? _____

7. How would you describe the mood of the music?

_____

8. What is the text about? _____

_____

9. Describe the ending of the song. How does it make you feel?

_____

_____

10. Describe the role of the piano in this song. _____

_____

iMusic Listening (Student Resource Disc)

Brahms: *Lullaby*

11. What is the form of this song? _____

12. What characteristic makes it sound like a lullaby?_____

_____

13. Is the melody mostly conjunct or disjunct?_____

14. Do you know this song? If yes, describe when you have heard it before.

_____

_____

---

54. *Review* The Nineteenth-Century Piano Piece and Its Composers
Chaps. 47–50, Sh 46–49

Exercises

True or False

____ 1. The piano became a popular instrument for amateur musicians.

____ 2. The piano changed little technically during the nineteenth century.

____ 3. The nineteenth century was an age of great virtuoso pianists.

4. Which nineteenth-century composers contributed to modern piano

technique? _____ _____

5. What are some of the descriptive titles that Romantic composers gave to

their piano works? _____

_____

6. Why is Chopin called the "poet of the piano"? _____

_____

7. What was Chopin's national heritage? _____

8. What is tempo rubato? _____

9. With which famous writer was Chopin romantically involved?

_____

10. In which small forms of piano music did Chopin write?

_____

In which large forms did he write? _____

Of these forms, which can be viewed as nationalistic?

_____

11. What music did Chopin write that did NOT include piano?

_____

*12. In which country was Franz Liszt born? _____

*13. With which famous writer was Liszt romantically involved?

_____

*14. What other aristocratic woman was important in Liszt's life?

_____

*15. What lifestyle did Liszt choose in his later years?_____

*16. Liszt devised a technique of developing a theme through constant variation of its melody, rhythm, or harmony. This process is known as _____.

*17. Which composer did Liszt describe as writing the "music of the future"?

_____

18. Describe Clara Schumann's early musical training.

_____
_____

19. In which musical genres did Clara Schumann write? _____

_____

20. What was her relationship with Robert Schumann? _____ with Brahms? _____

21. What was the public reaction to Clara Schumann as a pianist?

_____

22. What difficulties did a woman composer have in the nineteenth century?

_____
_____
_____
_____

55. *Listen* Chopin and Liszt: Romantic Masters of the Piano

Chopin: Polonaise in A major, Op. 40, No. 1 (*Military*) (**LG** 45, Sh 27, *e***LG**)
*Chopin: Prelude in E minor, Op. 28, No. 4 (**LG** 46, *e***LG**)
*Liszt: *The Little Bell* (*La campanella*) (**LG** 47, *e***LG**)

Exercises

Listen to Chopin's Polonaise in A minor, Op. 40, No. 1 while following the
Listening Guide, then answer questions 1–5 (check one).

1. This work is in:
   ___ a. duple meter.
   ___ b. triple meter.

2. The character of this polonaise is best described as:
   ___ a. heroic.
   ___ b. contemplative.

3. What is the overall form of this dance?
   ___ a. binary
   ___ b. ternary

4. Which is the typical polonaise rhythm (L = long; S = short)?
   ___ a. L SS SSSS
   ___ b. SL SL SSSS

5. Does the performance you heard use tempo rubato? _____

*Listen to Chopin's Prelude in E minor while following the Listening Guide,
then answer questions 6–11 (check one).

6. This prelude is a:
   ___ a. large-scale, multisectional work for piano.
   ___ b. small character work for piano.

7. The opening phrase of this prelude is:
   ___ a. disjunct with a wide range.
   ___ b. conjunct with a narrow range.

8. The work is performed with:
   ___ a. some freedom or rubato in the rhythm.
   ___ b. strict tempo and rhythm.

9. The meter is:
   ___ a. strong and dancelike in this work.
   ___ b. gentle and veiled in this work.

10. How would you characterize the mood of this work?

_____

11. Do you think this prelude is difficult to perform well? _____

    Explain. _____

*Listen to Liszt's *The Little Bell* while following the Listening Guide, then answer questions 12–15.

12. To which collection does *The Little Bell* belong? _____

    What is the purpose of these works? _____

    _____

13. On whose composition is this work based? _____

14. How does Liszt evoke the sound of a bell in this work?

    _____

    _____

    _____

15. What makes this work virtuosic (or very difficult to play)?

    _____

    _____

---

56. *Explore* Chopin in the Salon: From Paris to the Pacific
CP 10

Exercises

Complete the following questions.

1. What is the derivation of the word "salon"? _____

2. What is a salon concert? _____

   _____

3. Where did Chopin meet the writer George Sand? _____

   What is Sand's real name? _____

*4. In which cities was Chopin's music first published in America?

   _____

5. Which women musicians hosted musical salons in nineteenth-century

   Boston? _____

   _____

   _____

6. When was Chopin's music first performed in Mexico? _____

   In South America? _____

   When was the first biography of Chopin published in Latin America?

   _____

7. What movie depicts the popularity of the piano in New Zealand?

   _____

8. What role did women's clubs play in the spread of Chopin's music

   across America? _____

   _____

   _____

   _____

Listening Assignment

Select a piano work by Chopin (consider the *Minute Waltz* or the *Revolutionary Etude*), locate a recording of it in your campus library or through a music service, and write about its character. Imagine this work performed in a nineteenth-century Parisian salon concert and describe how people would react.

Or visit StudySpace (www.wwnorton.com/enjoy), read this Cultural Perspective, and follow links provided there. Write an essay describing your online research.

Selection: _____

Composer: _____

Describe the work: _____

_____

_____

_____

Describe the event: _____

_____

_____

_____

_____

_____

_____

_____

_____

_____

_____

_____

_____

_____

_____

_____

_____

_____

---

57. *Listen* **More Romantic Piano Music**

Clara Schumann: Nocturne, from *Music for an Evening Entertainment,* Op. 6
(**LG** 48, Sh 28, *e***LG**)
Louis Gottschalk: *The Banjo* (**LG** 49, Sh 29, *e***LG**)

Exercises

Listen to Clara Schumann's Nocturne while following the Listening Guide,
then answer questions 1–7.

1. What is the general character of a nocturne? _____

    _____

2. Does this nocturne fit your description above? _____ Explain.

    _____

    _____

3. Describe the mood of the contrasting middle section (**B**) of the work.

    _____

4. How does the return of the A section sound different from the

    opening? _____

5. How old was Clara Schumann when she wrote this set of character pieces

    (*Soirées musicales*)? _____ What other movements make up this

    collection? _____

6. What did Robert Schumann think about this particular nocturne?

    _____

    _____

7. In your opinion, is there anything about this work that seems

    "feminine"? _____ Explain. _____

    _____

Listen to Louis Gottschalk's *The Banjo* while following the Listening Guide,
then answer questions 8–13.

8. What American city was the home of composer Louis Gottschalk?

    _____

9. What are some of the well-known tunes that Gottschalk set in his piano

    works? _____

10. How did Gottschalk imitate a banjo in *The Banjo?* _____

    _____

11. Which famous nineteenth-century song did Gottschalk quote in the
    coda of *The Banjo?* _____

12. Which best describes the rhythmic character of *The Banjo?*
    ___ a. highly syncopated
    ___ b. lilting compound meter

13. The composer called this work a "grotesque fantasy." Which
    description below best fits this?
    ___ a. strict form and small-scale work
    ___ b. free form and large-scale work

iMusic Listening (Student Resource Disc)

Mendelssohn: *Spring Song*, Op. 62, No. 6

14. Describe how the performer uses rubato in this performance.

    _____

    _____

15. The melodic line in this work is:
    ___ a. conjunct.
    ___ b. disjunct.

16. What is the name for the broken chord accompaniment heard here?
    ___ a. arpeggio
    ___ b. ostinato

17. Have you heard this piano work previously? _____
    Describe the context or what images it brings to mind.

    _____

    _____

    _____

    _____

---

58. *Review* Romantic Program Music and Nationalism
Chaps. 51–53; Sh 49–51

Exercises

Match the following terms with their definitions.

a. absolute music	d. program music
b. concert overture	e. incidental music
c. program symphony	f. symphonic poem

_____ 1. Instrumental music that has some literary or pictorial association supplied by the composer.

_____ 2. Music lacking any literary or pictorial association.

_____ 3. A type of program music written to accompany plays.

_____ 4. A one-movement work for orchestra with a literary program.

_____ 5. A multimovement orchestral work with a literary program.

_____ 6. A one-movement work originally written to introduce a larger work but played independently.

Multiple Choice

_____ 7. Which composer is generally credited with the first use of the term "symphonic poem"?
    a. Franz Liszt
    b. Hector Berlioz
    c. Felix Mendelssohn

_____ 8. The chief difference between a symphonic poem and a program symphony is the:
    a. nature of the program.
    b. number of movements in the work.
    c. number of musicians involved.

9. Name a famous example of incidental music.

_____

10. What example of a program symphony did we study? _____

_____

11. In what ways do composers express their nationalism through music?

_____

_____

115

Match each composer with his national school.

a. Russian school   d. English school
b. Czech school   e. Spanish school
c. Scandinavian school

_____ 12. Jean Sibelius   ___ 16. Edvard Grieg

_____ 13. Bedřich Smetana   ___ 17. Alexander Borodin

_____ 14. Manuel de Falla   ___ 18. Edward Elgar

_____ 15. Peter Ilyich Tchaikovsky   ___ 19. Antonín Dvořák

20. The term "program music" can apply to music for film and television
as well as to nineteenth-century instrumental music. Briefly describe a
movie or television production you have seen recently and tell how the
music helped to tell the story or establish the mood.

Program: _____

_____

_____

_____

_____

_____

Musical description: _____

_____

_____

_____

_____

_____

_____

---

59. *Listen* Berlioz and Smetana

Berlioz: *Symphonie fantastique,* Fourth and *Fifth Movements (**LG** 50, Sh 30, *e***LG**)
Smetana: *The Moldau* (**LG** 51, Sh 31, *e***LG**)

Exercises

Listen to Berlioz's *Symphonie fantastique* while following the Listening Guide, then answer questions 1–9.

1. When and where did Berlioz write the *Symphonie fantastique?*

_____

2. What is "Romantic" about this work and its program?

_____

_____

_____

3. Who was the inspiration for this work?

_____

4. What is an *idée fixe* in music? _____

_____

5. How does Berlioz use this technique to unify his symphony?

_____

6. What is the mood of the March (fourth movement)?

_____

7. Can you hear the graphic musical "decapitation"? _____

What effect does it have? _____

*8. What effect does the use of the *Dies irae* chant have in the last

movement? _____

*9. What instruments are heard playing this theme?

_____

_____

_____

Listen to Smetana's *The Moldau* while following the Listening Guide, then answer questions 10–14.

_____ 10. Which type of program best describes *The Moldau?*
   a. literary, based on a play or novel
   b. philosophical, based on a conceptual idea
   c. graphic, depicting actual events or places

_____ 11. Which category of program music best describes *The Moldau?*
   a. program symphony
   b. symphonic poem
   c. incidental music

12. Which instruments does Smetana use to evoke the following?

   a. two streams joining: _____

   b. a flowing river: _____

   c. a hunting scene: _____

   d. moonlight on the water: _____

   e. memories of an ancient castle: _____

13. What circumstances might inspire a composer or artist to produce a nationalistic work?

   _____

   _____

   _____

14. Suggest an event or place that might inspire a modern-day nationalist composer.

   _____

   _____

   _____

   _____

---

60. *Explore* Music, Folklore, and Nationalism
CP 11

Exercises

Complete the following questions.

1. What lessons do folktales teach?_____

_____

_____

2. Cite a folktale you know and its moral or lesson.

_____

_____

_____

_____

3. Who is the Russian folk figure Baba-Yaga? _____

_____

_____

4. From which folk collection does the tale of "Hansel and Gretel" come?

_____

5. What is the source of the tale of "Aladdin"? _____

_____

   Of "Sleeping Beauty" and "Cinderella"? _____

_____

   Of "The Little Mermaid"? _____

6. What is the folk basis for Tchaikovsky's well-known ballet *The Nutcracker*?

_____

_____

7. What musical genres lend themselves to settings of folktales?

_____

Listening Assignment

Listen to one of the musical settings of folktales below. Familiarize yourself with the story (find the original tale or read over the recording notes) and describe below how the music portrays the events of the story.

Edvard Grieg, Incidental music to *Peer Gynt* (Norwegian legend)

Maurice Ravel, from *Mother Goose Suite* (*Ma mère l'oye*) (French tales by Perrault), one of the following movements: *Pavane de la Belle au bois dormant* (*Sleeping Beauty*) or *Petit Poucet* (*Tom Thumb*)

Peter Ilyich Tchaikovsky, *The Sleeping Beauty*, Op. 66a (ballet suite after Perrault tale)

Richard Strauss, *Till Eulenspiegel's Merry Pranks* (German tale)

Igor Stravinsky, *The Firebird* (Russian folktale)

Sergei Prokofiev, *Peter and the Wolf* (modern Russian tale) or *Cinderella* (ballet suite after Perrault tale)

Or visit StudySpace (www.wwnorton.com/enjoy), read this Cultural Perspective, and follow links provided there. Write an essay describing your online research.

_____

_____

_____

_____

_____

_____

_____

_____

_____

_____

_____

_____

_____

_____

_____

_____

_____

_____

_____

---

61. *Review* **Absolute Forms: The Symphony and the Concerto**
Chaps. 54, 57; Sh 53, 56

Terms to Remember

absolute music	scherzo
cadenza	sonata-allegro form
concerto	symphony
motive	theme
	tutti

Exercises

Complete the following questions.

1. The symphony is a large-scale work for orchestra, made up of several

   independent parts, or _____.

2. The symphony first became an important form in the _____

   era.

3. Three composers in Vienna who mastered the form and handed it

   down to Romantic composers were _____,

   _____, and _____.

4. The symphony cycle typically has _____ movements.

5. Of these, the _____ movement is usually the most highly

   structured, and features the use of _____ form.

6. What forms are typical for the second movement of a symphony?

   _____

Multiple Choice

____ 7. Which is the most typical tempo structure for a symphony?
   a. fast, moderate triple dance, slow, fast
   b. slow, fast, fast, moderate triple dance
   c. fast, slow, moderate triple dance, fast

____ 8. The third movement of the nineteenth-century symphony is
   usually in:
   a. scherzo form.
   b. sonata-allegro form.
   c. theme and variations form.

_____ 9. The concerto most typically has:
   a. one movement.
   b. three movements.
   c. four movements.

10. In what ways did nineteenth-century composers change the overall form of the symphony? _____

_____

11. How does the form of the first movement of a concerto differ from sonata-allegro form in a symphony? _____

_____

_____

12. Who were some of the major contributors to the Romantic concerto?

_____

13. How do you account for the rise in virtuosity in the nineteenth century?

_____

_____

14. Since absolute forms such as the symphony and the concerto generally have no program, what gives them their sense of shape and meaning?

_____

_____

_____

---

62. *Listen* Brahms and Dvořák as Symphonists
Brahms: Symphony No. 3 in F major, Third Movement (**LG** 52, Sh 32, *e***LG**)
*Dvořák: Symphony No. 9 in E minor, First Movement (**LG** 53, *e***LG**)

Exercises

Listen to the third movement of Brahms's Symphony No. 3 while following the Listening Guide, then answer questions 1–7.

1. How many symphonies did Brahms write? _____

   Why did he wait until late in his life to write symphonies?

   _____

   _____

2. What is the composer's musical motto, heard in Symphony No. 3?

   _____

3. How many movements does this symphony have? _____

4. What is unusual about the third movement? _____

   _____

5. How would you describe the musical character of this third movement's:

   opening section? _____

   middle section? _____

6. What is changed in the restatement (return of opening theme)?

   _____

7. How is this symphony cyclical? _____

   _____

   Name another cyclical symphony.

   _____

*Listen to the first movement of Dvořák's Symphony No. 9 (*From the New World*) while following the Listening Guide, then answer questions 8–14.

8. How did this symphony get its subtitle *From the New World?*

   _____

9. What is "American" about the work? _____

   _____

10. On what epic poem is it loosely based? _____

    _____ Who is the poet? _____

11. Is this symphony in standard sonata-cycle form? _____

    Are the keys of the movements standard? _____

12. How has Dvořák achieved a folklike character in the themes of the first

    movement? _____

    _____

13. What works did Dvořák write that could be considered nationalistic?

    _____

    _____

14. Describe the mood or picture you envision when you listen to this
    movement of the *New World* Symphony.

    _____

    _____

    _____

---

63. *Explore* Dvořák's Influence on African-American Art Music
CP 12

Exercises

Complete the following questions.

1. What types of traditional music interested Dvořák during his years in America? _____

   _____

2. What famous American poem is loosely the basis for Dvořák's *New World* Symphony?_____

3. Which spiritual did Dvořák like especially?

   _____

4. What challenge did Dvořák issue to American composers?

   _____

   _____

   _____

*5. For what is Dvořák's student Henry Burleigh known today?

   _____

   _____

   _____

6. Which well-known African-American composer rose to Dvořák's challenge? _____

   How did he accomplish this? _____

   _____

   _____

   _____

*7. Which white American composer is famous for his wedding of jazz to art music? _____

   Which work demonstrates this? _____

Listening Assignment

Listen to a recording of one movement from William Grant Still's *Afro-American Symphony* and describe how it imitates blues, jazz, spirituals, or other traditional African-American music styles and instruments. (Or listen to Still's Suite for Violin and Piano, third movement; Gershwin's *Rhapsody in Blue* or Concerto in F; or an arrangement for a spiritual.) Consider what musical elements of African-American music influenced this work.

Or visit StudySpace (www.wwnorton.com/enjoy), read this Cultural Perspective, and follow links provided there. Write an essay describing your online research.

Selection: _____

Composer: _____

_____

_____

_____

_____

_____

_____

_____

_____

_____

_____

_____

_____

_____

_____

_____

_____

_____

_____

_____

_____

---

64. *Listen* Felix Mendelssohn and the Romantic Concerto
*Felix Mendelssohn: Violin Concerto in E minor, Op. 64, First Movement
(**LG** 54, *e***LG**)

Exercises

*Listen to the first movement of Felix Mendelssohn's Violin Concerto in
E minor while following the Listening Guide, then answer the following
questions.

1. What is the tempo scheme for the movements of this concerto?

   _____

   Does this fit the Classical scheme? _____

2. What is unusual about the form of the first movement? _____

   _____

3. Is there an orchestral exposition? _____

4. How would you describe the first theme? _____

   _____

5. Where does the cadenza occur? _____

   Is this the normal place? _____

6. Is there a break before the second movement? _____

7. For whom was this concerto written? _____

8. Was the cadenza improvised or written by the composer?

   _____

9. What effect does the minor key have on the character of the first

   movement? _____

   _____

10. What are some Classical elements of this work? _____

    _____

    _____

11. What are some Romantic elements? _____

    _____

    _____

*12. What was Mendelssohn's early family life like? _____

_____

How did his upbringing contribute to his love of music?

_____

*13. Which earlier composers did Mendelssohn revere?

_____

*14. Which major work by a Baroque composer did he revive?

_____

15. Besides composing, what other musical roles did Mendelssohn take on?

_____

16. Which famous conservatory did he found? _____

17. Mendelssohn died at a very young age, just months after the premature
death of which beloved family member? _____

*18. What other orchestral works did Mendelssohn write? _____

_____

*19. His most famous incidental music, based on Shakespeare, was

_____

*20. Name a well-known oratorio by Mendelssohn. _____

*21. In which other genres did he compose? _____

_____

---

65. *Review* **The Rise of Classical Composition in America**
Chap. 59, Sh 50
*Amy Beach: Violin Sonata in A minor, Second Movement (**LG** 55, *e***LG**)

Exercises

Complete the following questions.

1. What musical tradition prevailed in America in the nineteenth century?

   _____

2. Which European singer was known as the "Swedish nightingale"?

   _____

3. Name two prominent New England composers who also held
   important university professorships. Cite one work by each.

   Composer: _____   _____

   University: _____   _____

   Work: _____   _____

4. Which composer set Native-American tunes in his music?

   _____

5. Who was the most prominent woman composer of the New England

   School? _____ Name several of her works.

   _____

6. What composition inspired Beach's Symphony in E minor?

   _____

7. Why is her symphony significant?

   _____

8. What folk styles did she incorporate into this symphony?

   _____

*9. Which of her works reflect her interest in bird songs?

   _____

*10. Where did she write these piano works?

   _____

11. Why did she prefer to be known as Mrs. H. H. A. Beach?

   _____

*Listen to the second movement of Amy Beach's Violin Sonata in A minor while following the Listening Guide, then answer questions 12–21.

12. When was this sonata written? _____

13. Where and by whom was it premiered? _____

_____

14. What was the reaction of critics to the sonata? _____

_____

15. Does the sonata generally conform to the multimovement cycle?

_____

16. Is it normal for the second movement to be a scherzo? _____

17. Is it normal for a scherzo to be set in duple meter? _____

18. Describe the opening theme of the scherzo.

_____

19. Describe the mood of the trio. _____

_____

20. What is a perpetuum mobile? _____

Does this phrase apply to this movement? _____

21. What European composer's techniques seem to have influenced Beach in this sonata? _____ What techniques?

_____

---

66. *Explore* **Women and Music: A Feminist Perspective**
CP 13

Exercises

Complete the following questions.

1. What was the typical nineteenth-century attitude toward women and
   their artistic creativity? _____

   _____

2. Name two female novelists and the pen names under which they wrote.

   _____

   _____

3. What were the concerns of the women's movement in the early twentieth
   century? _____

4. When did women gain the right to vote? _____

5. What contributions did composer Ethel Smyth make to the women's
   movement? _____

   _____

6. Which modern women composers have focused on the experiences of
   women? _____

7. What has been the general attitude toward women in popular music?

   _____

   _____

8. Which modern performers have tried to stop "female bashing" in
   popular music? _____

9. Do you think there is a "women's voice" expressed in music? _____
   Why or why not? _____

   _____

10. Do you think that biology, or gender, plays a role in the creative process?
    _____ Explain. _____

    _____

Listening Assignment

Select a recording of a modern female performer or of music by a modern female composer. Listen to the lyrics or read about the work and its inspiration. Comment below on whether there is a "woman's voice" being expressed.

Or visit StudySpace (www.wwnorton.com/enjoy), read the Cultural Perspective, and follow links provided there. Write an essay describing your online research.

_____

_____

_____

_____

_____

_____

_____

_____

_____

_____

_____

_____

_____

_____

_____

_____

_____

_____

_____

_____

_____

_____

_____

_____

---

67. *Listen* Romantic Choral Music
Brahms: *A German Requiem,* Fourth Movement (**LG** 56, Sh 33, *e***LG**)
Fanny Mendelssohn Hensel: *Under the Greenwood Tree* (**LG** 57, Sh 34, *e***LG**)

Exercises

Listen to the fourth movement of *A German Requiem* by Brahms while
following the Listening Guide, then answer questions 1–7.

1. What events in Brahms's life inspired him to write a requiem?

   _____

2. In what language is a Requiem Mass usually sung? _____

   With which church is it usually associated? _____

3. Rather than using the standard text of the Requiem Mass, Brahms
   constructed his own. What sources did he use?

   _____

   _____

   _____

   _____

4. What musical forces does it take to perform *A German Requiem?*

   _____

   _____

5. What is the text source for the fourth movement? _____

   From which part of the Bible is this text taken? _____

6. What is the mood established by this movement? _____

   How does Brahms suggest this character through music?

   _____

   _____

7. What unifies the fourth movement of this Requiem?

   _____

   _____

Listen to the part song *Under the Greenwood Tree* by Fanny Mendelssohn
Hensel, then answer questions 8–10.

8. What was the source of the text for this song? _____

9. How many verses are heard in the song? _____ How many times is the chorus heard? _____

10. What is the text about in this song? _____

_____

Complete the following questions.

11. What factors contributed to the rise of amateur choral groups in the nineteenth century? _____

_____

_____

12. What are the main choral forms used in the nineteenth century?

_____

13. What are the standard voice parts in a choir? _____

14. What is a part song? _____

_____

15. Which Romantic composers contributed significantly to the choral music literature? _____

16. What skills does singing in a choir require? _____

_____

Do you have any choral singing experience? _____

If so, with which group(s)? _____

_____

68. *Explore* Music and Shakespeare
CP 14

Exercises

Complete the following questions.

1. What is a ballad and what subjects did ballads treat? _____

   _____

2. Name several Shakespeare plays that feature songs. _____

   _____

3. From which Shakespeare play did Fanny Mendelssohn take the text for

   her part song *Under the Greenwood Tree*? _____

4. What famous Shakespeare play is the basis for the musical *West Side*

   Story? _____

5. What other musical works were inspired by this same play? _____

   _____

6. Name three Verdi operas based on Shakespeare plays:

   a. _____

   b. _____

   c. _____

7. What recent movie presented the life of the bard Shakespeare?

   _____

8. Which Shakespeare play has been updated in a rap version?

   _____

   What is the adaptation titled? _____

Activity

Watch a movie version of Bernstein's musical *West Side Story* (from your library or video store) and discuss how the plot updates Shakespeare's story of Romeo and Juliet.

Or visit StudySpace (www.wwnorton.com/enjoy), read the Cultural Perspective, and follow links provided there. Write an essay describing your online research.

69. *Review* Romantic Opera
Chap. 62–65, Sh 58–60

Exercises

Complete the following questions.

1. Describe the following parts of an opera, giving consideration to musical style and purpose within the plot. You may wish to refer back to an earlier chapter.

   a. aria: _____

   _____

   b. recitative: _____

   _____

   c. chorus: _____

   _____

   d. ensemble: _____

   _____

2. What is the role of the orchestra in an opera? _____

   _____

3. What is a libretto, and who writes it? _____

   _____

Match the following styles of opera with their definitions.

_____ 4. grand opera   a. light German opera featuring spoken dialogue

_____ 5. opéra comique   b. Italian version of comic opera

_____ 6. Singspiel   c. a genre that integrates music and theater

_____ 7. opera seria   d. French opera style, featuring historical subjects and huge forces

_____ 8. opera buffa   e. Italian singing style featuring florid lines and pure voices

_____ 9. bel canto   f. French comic opera, with simple plots and spoken dialogue

_____ 10. music drama   g. Italian serious opera

Match the following well-known operas with their composers (look up the principal works of these composers in the text or on StudySpace).

_____ 11. *Die Meistersinger von Nürnberg*   a. Giuseppe Verdi

_____ 12. *Aida*   b. Richard Wagner

_____ 13. *La traviata*

_____ 14. *Siegfried*

_____ 15. *Tristan and Isolde*

_____ 16. *The Flying Dutchman*

_____ 17. *Otello*

18. What makes an opera "exotic"? _____

    _____

    Name an example. _____

19. Name an opera composed by a woman. _____

    Who was the composer? _____

    What was the basis of the plot? _____

20. Which famous tenor was also a celebrated singing teacher?

    _____

21. What was the relationship between Maria Malibran and Pauline Viardot?

    _____

22. For which operas were each of these singers known?

    _____

    _____

23. Did opera further the careers of women musicians in the Romantic

    era? _____ Explain. _____

    _____

    _____

70. *Listen* Verdi and Wagner
Verdi: *Rigoletto*, Act III, excerpt (**LG** 58, Sh 35, *e***LG**)
Wagner: *Die Walküre*, Act III, *Ride* and *Finale (**LG** 59, Sh 36, *e***LG**)

Exercises

Listen to the excerpt from Verdi's *Rigoletto* while following the Listening Guide, then answer questions 1–6.

1. What literary work provided the basis for *Rigoletto?*

_____

2. When and where is the story of *Rigoletto* set? _____

_____

3. Describe the melodic style of the aria "La donna è mobile."

_____

4. What is the Duke's attitude toward women? _____

_____

5. Describe the emotions each character is expressing in the quartet.

    The Duke: _____

    Maddalena: _____

    Gilda: _____

    Rigoletto: _____

6. Why do you think Verdi's operas have remained so popular?

_____

ABOUT THE COMPOSER

7. In what country was Verdi born? _____

8. Which Verdi operas were inspired by Shakespeare?

_____

9. Which of his operas could be described as "exotic"?

_____

10. What was his last great opera? _____

Listen to the excerpt from Wagner's *Die Walküre* while following the Listening Guide, then answer questions 11–23.

11. What is the basis for the story of this opera? _____

12. Who is Wotan? _____

    Brünnhilde? _____

13. What is happening in the opera during the famous *Ride of the Valkyries?*

    _____

    _____

*14. Describe the following musical themes in your own words.

    Wotan's farewell: _____

    Wotan's invocation of Loge: _____

    "Magic fire" music: _____

    "Magic sleep" music: _____

True or False

____ 15. Wagner's operas reflect his desire to link music and drama closely.

____ 16. His operas have the same individual components—arias, recitatives, and ensembles—as Verdi's.

____ 17. *The Ring of the Nibelung* is a cycle of four operas.

____ 18. Wagner strove to achieve an endless melody that was melded to the German language.

____ 19. The orchestra was unimportant to Wagner's music dramas.

____ 20. Wagner employed recurring themes called leitmotifs.

____ 21. Wagner's harmonic style was a conservative, diatonic one.

22. What music festival was established for the performance of Wagner's

    operas? _____

23. With whom did Wagner find happiness late in his life?

    _____

71. *Listen* Late Romantic Opera and Exoticism
*Bizet: *Carmen*, Act I, excerpt (**LG** 60, *e***LG**)
 Puccini: *Madame Butterfly*, "Un bel dì" (**LG** 61, Sh 37, *e***LG**)
 *Japanese Kouta: *A White Fan* (**LG** 62, *e***LG**)

Exercises

*Listen to the excerpt from Bizet's *Carmen* while following the Listening Guide, then answer questions 1–8.

1. What is the literary basis for *Carmen*? _____

_____

2. In which language is *Carmen* written? _____

3. What role does the chorus play in Act I of *Carmen*?

_____

_____

4. What kind of rhythmic accompaniment is heard in Carmen's aria?

_____

5. What is seductive about her character and her music?

_____

_____

6. Is Carmen a likable character? _____ Explain. _____

_____

7. What gives this opera its dramatic impact? _____

_____

8. In your opinion, what accounts for the popularity of this opera?

_____

_____

Listen to "Un bel dì" from Puccini's *Madame Butterfly* while following the Listening Guide, then answer questions 9–15.

9. What is the basis for Puccini's opera *Madame Butterfly*?

_____

_____

10. At what point in the story does Butterfly sing the aria "Un bel dì"?

_____

_____

11. What gives this aria its highly dramatic mood? _____

_____

12. How does *Madame Butterfly* end? _____

_____

13. What is exotic about *Madame Butterfly*? _____

_____

14. What other composers carried on the late-Romantic Italian operatic

tradition? _____

15. What was the movement known as *verismo*? _____

_____

*Listen to the Japanese kouta *A White Fan* (*Hakusen no*) while following the
Listening Guide, then answer questions 16–21.

16. What is a geisha?_____

_____

What would be the closest Western equivalent? _____

17. What kind of musical training was essential for a Japanese geisha?

_____

_____

18. What is a kouta? _____

19. For what occasion(s) would the kouta *A White Fan* be sung?

_____

20. Describe the vocal line of *A White Fan.* _____

_____

21. What instrument accompanies the voice in this song? _____

How is it played?_____

_____

72. *Review* Tchaikovsky and the Ballet
Chap. 67, Sh 62

Exercises

True or False

_____ 1. Renaissance entertainments included elaborate dance sequences as part of theatrical productions.

_____ 2. Classical ballet was first developed in the Romantic era by the Russians.

_____ 3. Stravinsky and Diaghilev were famous Russian dancers.

_____ 4. The *pas de deux*, or dance for two, developed in Russia by the choreographer Petipa, is a standard element of classical ballet.

_____ 5. Tchaikovsky and Petipa worked together on *The Nutcracker*.

Complete the following questions.

6. What three well-known ballets did Tchaikovsky write?

   a. _____

   b. _____

   c. _____

7. *The Nutcracker* was based on a story originally written by the Romantic

   writer _____ and later expanded by

   _____.

ABOUT THE COMPOSER

8. What teaching position did Tchaikovsky hold in Russia?

_____

9. How did Tchaikovsky feel about his homosexuality?

_____

10. What role did Nadezhda von Meck play in the composer's life?

_____

11. What was the reaction of Western audiences to Tchaikovsky's music?

_____

_____

143

12. In addition to ballet, in which other musical genres did Tchaikovsky write? _____

_____

THE NUTCRACKER

13. What is the setting for *The Nutcracker?* _____

_____

14. Who are the main characters? _____

_____

15. How do the "exotic" Arab and Chinese dances fit into the story of the ballet? _____

_____

16. How does Tchaikovsky set a different mood for each dance?

_____

17. Describe the character of each of the following dances.

    March: _____

    Dance of the Sugar Plum Fairy: _____

_____

    Trepak: _____

18. Have you ever seen a performance of *The Nutcracker?* _____

    If yes, was it ___ live, ___ on TV, or ___ on video?

    Did you enjoy it? _____

    What do you think accounts for the continued popularity of this classical ballet? _____

_____

_____

144

73. *Review* The Post-Romantic Era and Impressionism
Trans. IV, Chap. 68, Sh 63

Exercises

Complete the following questions.

1. Give the approximate dates of the post-Romantic era. _____

2. Which Italian operatic composers can be associated with post-

   Romanticism? _____

3. Which Germanic composers can be associated with post-Romanticism?

   _____

4. Which composer was most influential in the harmonic language of

   post-Romanticism? _____

5. Which post-Romantic composer was an important symphonist?

   _____

Multiple Choice

_____ 6. Which is NOT true of the origins of Impressionism?
   a. It was first a term denoting scorn of the new style.
   b. The coining of the term was based on a painting by Claude Monet.
   c. The style was first popular in Italy.
   d. A school of artists developed, all wishing to capture first
      impressions on canvas.

_____ 7. Who among these is NOT an Impressionist painter?
   a. Paul Klee   c. Edgar Degas
   b. Claude Monet   d. Auguste Renoir

_____ 8. In poetry, the parallel movement toward suggestion rather than
      direct description was:
   a. Expressionism.   c. Symbolism.
   b. New Romanticism.   d. minimalism.

_____ 9. Which American poet strongly influenced the literary movement
      referred to in the previous question?
   a. Thomas Jefferson   c. Stéphane Mallarmé
   b. Edgar Allan Poe   d. Paul Verlaine

10. What were some goals of Impressionist painters? _____

   _____

   _____

11. Describe the characteristics of Impressionist painting in your own words, based on the Monet painting *Impression: Sun Rising*, reproduced in your text. _____

_____

_____

12. Characterize the musical elements of Impressionist music below.

Melody/scales: _____

_____

Rhythm/meter: _____

_____

Harmony/dissonance: _____

_____

Form: _____

_____

13. In what ways did non-Western music influence Impressionism?

_____

_____

14. In what ways did Impressionism look back to earlier musical styles?

_____

_____

15. Which composer best exemplifies musical Impressionism?

_____

---

74. *Listen* Mahler, Debussy, and Ravel
*Mahler: *The Song of the Earth,* Third Movement (**LG** 64, *e***LG**)
 Debussy: *Prelude to "The Afternoon of a Faun"* (**LG** 65, Sh 39, *e***LG**)
*Ravel: Two songs from *Don Quixote to Dulcinea* (**LG** 66, *e***LG**)

Exercises

*Listen to the third movement from Mahler's *The Song of the Earth* while following the Listening Guide, then answer questions 1–4.

1. What is the literary basis for *The Song of the Earth*?

_____

2. What is the medium (performing forces) for this song cycle?

_____

3. How does Mahler evoke the sounds of Chinese music in this work?

_____

_____

4. How does the text evoke images of China? _____

_____

Listen to Debussy's *Prelude to "The Afternoon of a Faun"* while following the Listening Guide, then answer questions 5–9.

5. What is the literary source for this Debussy work?

_____

6. Briefly summarize the program for this work. _____

_____

_____

7. In your opinion, how does Debussy evoke images from the poem

   musically? _____

_____

_____

8. What Impressionistic traits do you hear in this work?

   Melody/rhythm: _____

   Harmony/texture: _____

   Form: _____

Timbre/color: _____

Other: _____

9. How does Debussy slightly vary the return of the opening material?

_____

_____

*Listen to the two songs from Ravel's song cycle *Don Quixote to Dulcinea* while following the Listening Guide, then answer questions 10–18.

10. What is the literary basis for this song cycle?

Author: _____ Title: _____

11. Who are the two characters mentioned in the song cycle's title?

_____

12. What Broadway musical is based on this same literary subject?

_____

13. Which dance rhythm is heard in the *Romanesque Song?* _____

Describe its character. _____

14. Which dance rhythm is heard in the *Drinking Song?* _____

Describe its character. _____

15. How did Ravel know these Spanish dance types? _____

_____

_____ 16. Which best describes the form of the *Drinking Song?*

a. through-composed   b. strophic with refrain   c. binary

_____ 17. Which singing style is evoked in the *Drinking Song?*

a. Gregorian chant   b. Sprechtsimme   c. flamenco

18. List some other works by Ravel that were inspired by the musics of other cultures. _____

_____

_____

75. *Explore* The Paris World Exhibition of 1889: A Cultural Awakening
CP 15

Exercises

Complete the following questions.

1. What famous monument was built for the Paris World Exhibition of 1889? _____

2. What is a gamelan orchestra? _____

_____

_____

From where did the gamelan that Debussy heard come?_____

3. What elements of gamelan music did Debussy try to imitate in his compositions? _____

_____

_____

4. Which other countries were represented by musicians at this world exhibition? _____

_____

_____

5. What Middle Eastern styles of dancing were seen at this event?

_____

6. What is a cakewalk? _____

_____

Where did it originate? _____

7. What other traditional music styles influenced Debussy?

_____

_____

8. What world music styles influenced the composer Maurice Ravel?

_____

_____

149

iMusic Listening Assignment (Student Resource Disc)

Listen to the iMusic recording of the gamelan piece *Tabuh Kenilu Sawik*.
Which country is the gamelan from? What are the instruments heard?
Describe how they sound and comment on the musical style (melody,
rhythm, harmony, texture).

Or visit StudySpace (www.wwnorton.com/enjoy), read the Cultural Perspective, and follow links provided there. Write an essay describing your online
research.

---

76. *Review* Elements of Twentieth-Century Musical Style
Chaps. 70–71, Sh 64–65

Exercises

Multiple Choice

_____ 1. In which element of music was primitivism most evident?
    a. melody
    b. rhythm
    c. texture
    d. harmony

_____ 2. Which statement is NOT true of Expressionism?
    a. It was principally a French movement.
    b. It attempted to probe the subconscious.
    c. It defied traditional notions of beauty.
    d. It portrayed images in distortion.

_____ 3. Which is most typical of Expressionist music?
    a. conjunct, symmetrical melodies
    b. instruments used in extreme high and low registers
    c. consonant, tonal harmonies
    d. regular meters and rhythms

_____ 4. Which is most typical of the New Classicism?
    a. an emotional, expressive style
    b. a focus on program music
    c. a preference for absolute music
    d. an attempt to bring music and poetry closer

Match the following early-twentieth-century figures with their correct descriptions.

_____ 5. Paul Gauguin   a. Expressionist composer

_____ 6. Pablo Picasso   b. Expressionist writer

_____ 7. Franz Kafka   c. Expressionist painter

_____ 8. Joan Miró   d. French painter drawn to primitive subjects

_____ 9. Arnold Schoenberg   e. Surrealist painter

_____ 10. Oskar Kokoschka   f. Cubist painter

11. What contributions did composer Arnold Schoenberg make to music in this era? _____

Match the following musical terms with their definitions.

_____ 12. polyrhythm   a. a particular arrangement of the twelve chromatic tones

_____ 13. dissonant counterpoint   b. the use of two or more keys together

_____ 14. polytonality   c. music based on the twelve-tone method

_____ 15. serial music   d. the simultaneous use of several rhythmic patterns

_____ 16. tone row   e. the use of dissonant intervals to set musical lines apart

_____ 17. atonality   f. the rejection of any key or tonality

True or False

_____ 18. In twentieth-century music, dissonances do not always resolve.

_____ 19. Orchestras grew even larger in the early twentieth century.

_____ 20. Twentieth-century melodies are generally more difficult to sing than those of the Romantic era.

_____ 21. The use of triads continued to predominate early-twentieth-century music.

_____ 22. Schoenberg is generally credited with founding the twelve-tone method of composition.

_____ 23. Tone rows were often transposed to other pitch levels.

_____ 24. Early-twentieth-century music remained consonant to the ear.

_____ 25. Duple, triple, and quadruple meter were the norm in the early twentieth century.

_____ 26. Inversion refers to the mirror-image movement of a line, wherein each interval moves in the opposite direction from the original.

_____ 27. Dark or low instruments were explored by early-twentieth-century composers.

77. *Listen* The Music of Stravinsky
Stravinsky: *The Rite of Spring*, Part I, excerpts (**LG** 67, Sh 40, *e***LG**)
*Stravinsky: *The Royal March*, from *The Soldier's Tale* (**LG** 68, *e***LG**)

Exercises

Listen to the excerpts from Stravinsky's *The Rite of Spring* while following the Listening Guide, then answer questions 1–6.

1. Name the three ballets Stravinsky composed for Diaghilev and the

   Ballets Russes. _____

   _____

2. Name three musical characteristics of *The Rite of Spring* that shaped a

   new musical language for the twentieth century. _____

   _____

   _____

3. What makes *The Rite of Spring* a nationalistic work?

   _____

   _____

   _____

4. Describe how Stravinsky expanded the orchestra in *The Rite of Spring*.

   _____

   _____

5. Describe the story of the ballet, in particular the action in Part I.

   _____

   _____

   _____

   _____

6. How does Stravinsky evoke primitivism in *The Rite of Spring*?

   _____

   _____

   _____

*Listen to *The Royal March* from Stravinsky's *The Soldier's Tale*, then answer questions 7–10.

    7. What is the literary basis for *The Soldier's Tale?* _____

_____

    8. What is Neoclassical about this work?_____

_____

    9. Describe the rhythmic nature of *The Royal March* from *The Soldier's Tale.*

_____

_____

    10. What is the form of *The Royal March?* _____

ABOUT THE COMPOSER

    11. Where was Stravinsky born? _____

    12. Where was *The Rite of Spring* premiered? _____

    13. Where did Stravinsky live after World War I? _____

    After World War II? _____

    14. Late in life, Stravinsky wrote twelve-tone compositions. Name one:

_____

    15. Name a choral work by Stravinsky:_____

    An opera: _____

---

78. *Listen* **Schoenberg, Berg, and Webern**
Schoenberg: *Pierrot lunaire*, Nos. 18 and *21 (**LG** 69, Sh 41, *e***LG**)
*Berg: *Wozzeck*, Act III, excerpts (**LG** 70, *e***LG**)
*Webern: Symphony, Op. 21, Second Movement (**LG** 71, *e***LG**)

Exercises

Listen to the selections from Schoenberg's *Pierrot lunaire* while following the Listening Guide, then answer questions 1–9.

1. What new singing style did Schoenberg employ in *Pierrot lunaire*?

   _____ Describe this style. _____

   _____

   What were Schoenberg's goals in using this style? _____

   _____

2. What is the literary source of the poems in *Pierrot lunaire*?

   _____

3. What is the performance medium for this work? _____

   _____

4. With what is the main character preoccupied in these poems?

   _____

5. What is Expressionistic about this work? _____

   _____

6. Describe the harmony and texture of *The Moonfleck* (No. 18).

   _____

*7. How are these elements treated in *O Scent of Fabled Yesteryear* (No. 21)?

   _____

8. Schoenberg abandoned the traditional ordering of a work around a key

   center, resulting first in a style known as _____.

   He eventually devised a system using all twelve tones of the chromatic

   scale, known as _____. In which period does *Pierrot*

   lunaire fall? _____

9. What was the relationship of Schoenberg to composers Alban Berg and

   Anton Webern? _____

*Listen to the excerpt from Berg's opera *Wozzeck* while following the Listening Guide, then answer questions 10–14.

10. What is the literary basis for the opera *Wozzeck?*

_____

11. What is Expressionistic about its subject and music?

_____

_____

12. How does the vocal line portray Wozzeck's state of mind?

_____

13. What is the emotional effect of the opera's closing scene?

_____

14. What was Berg's other opera? _____

*Listen to the second movement from Webern's Symphony, Op. 21, while following the Listening Guide, then answer questions 15–20.

15. What size orchestra does this work employ?_____

16. What is *Klangfarbenmelodie?* _____

_____

How does this technique compare with pointillism in painting?

_____

17. What contrapuntal procedures occur in this movement?

_____

_____

18. Is this work _____ tonal, _____ atonal, or _____ serial?

19. What formal structures are employed in the work? _____

_____

20. How did Webern die? _____

_____

---

79. *Review* Nationalism in the Twentieth Century
Chaps. 76–77, Sh 68–69

Exercises

Match the following composers with their nationalistic schools on the right.
You may use answers as many times as necessary.

_____	1. Benjamin Britten	a. French school
_____	2. Paul Hindemith	b. German school
_____	3. Charles Ives	c. Russian school
_____	4. Sergei Rachmaninoff	d. English school
_____	5. Béla Bartók	e. Hungarian school
_____	6. Carl Orff	f. Scandinavian school
_____	7. Dmitri Shostakovich	g. American school
_____	8. Francis Poulenc	h. Spanish school
_____	9. Jean Sibelius	
_____	10. Sergei Prokofiev	
_____	11. Manuel de Falla	

12. For each of the countries below, suggest a historical event or nationalistic theme or setting that either served or could have served as the basis for a musical composition.

    a. Russia: _____

    b. France: _____

    c. Germany: _____

    d. England: _____

    e. United States: _____

13. What were the goals of the French group known as *Les Six?*

_____

*14. Name a composer and work linked to Jewish cultural origins.

_____

_____

True or False

_____ 15. Shape-note notation was designed for people who could not read music.

_____ 16. The American composer Charles Ives was from California.

_____ 17. William Grant Still was the first African-American composer to have a symphony performed by a major American symphony orchestra.

18. For what types of music is Stephen Foster known? Name three of his works. _____

_____

19. Out of what tradition did American bands grow?

_____

20. Who was America's most famous bandmaster? _____

Name two marches he composed. _____

_____

21. Which famous musical instrument inventor revolutionized the keys on brass instruments?_____

What well-known instrument did he invent? _____

22. Which New England composer was inspired by the hymns and patriotic songs he learned as a youth?_____

23. With which cultural movement is William Grant Still associated?

_____

24. How did Still break down racial barriers?_____

_____

_____

---

80. *Explore* **Bartók—A Folk-Song Collector**
CP 16

Exercises

Complete the following questions.

1. What were Béla Bartók's goals in collecting Eastern European folk songs?

   _____

   _____

   _____

2. What is an ethnomusicologist? _____

   _____

3. How was Bartók's art music influenced by the traditional music he

   collected? _____

   _____

   _____

4. What is an additive meter? _____

   _____

   _____

*5. Describe the background of the Roma people and their musical

   traditions. _____

   _____

   _____

   _____

6. What are Roma people popularly called? _____

7. What was the makeup of a Roma band? _____

8. What nineteenth-century Hungarian composer was interested in Roma

   music? _____ What evidence do we have

   of this interest? _____

   _____

Listening Assignment

Listen to a recording of modern Roma music (find one in your library or ask your instructor for one from the Music Example Bank). Name the ensemble selected, list the instruments heard, and describe the musical style (melodic, rhythmic, harmonic, and singing styles).

Or visit StudySpace (www.wwnorton.com/enjoy), read the Cultural Perspective, and follow links provided there. Write an essay describing your online research.

_____

_____

_____

_____

_____

_____

_____

_____

_____

_____

_____

_____

_____

_____

_____

_____

_____

_____

_____

_____

_____

_____

_____

_____

81. *Listen* Bartók and Ives

Bartók: *Concerto for Orchestra*, Fourth Movement (**LG** 72, Sh 42, *e***LG**)
*Ives: *The Things Our Fathers Loved* (**LG** 73, *e***LG**)

Exercises

Listen to *Interrupted Intermezzo* from Bartók's *Concerto for Orchestra* while following the Listening Guide, then answer questions 1–8.

1. How can this orchestral work be a concerto even though it has no solo instrument? _____

_____

2. When was it written? _____ Who commissioned it?

_____

3. How many movements does the *Concerto for Orchestra* have? _____

4. What elements of folk music are captured in this work?

_____

5. From which composer and work does Bartók borrow a theme in the fourth movement? _____

6. What is the general form of the fourth movement? _____

7. How would you describe the meter of the opening? _____

_____

8. Is Bartók's music dissonant? _____ What is the effect?

_____

ABOUT THE COMPOSER

9. What nationality was Bartók? _____

10. What attracted him to the folk music of his native land?

_____

_____

11. Name several of Bartók's most famous compositions.

_____

_____

12. Why did Bartók leave his homeland and come to America?

_____

161

*Listen to *The Things Our Fathers Loved* by Ives while following the Listening Guide, then answer questions 13–18.

13. What tunes does Ives incorporate into this song?

    _____

    _____

    Which of the tunes do you recognize? _____

    _____

14. How is Ives's music nationalistic? _____

    _____

    _____

15. How would you characterize his treatment of harmony?

    _____

16. What familiar American images does this song bring to mind?

    _____

    _____

17. What are some of Ives's other nationalistic compositions?

    _____

    _____

18. Charles Ives is viewed today as one of the great twentieth-century American composers. How was his music received by the public during his lifetime?

    _____

    _____

┌───┐
│ **82.** *Explore* **Music and the Patriotic Spirit**   │
│ CP 17   │
└───┘

Exercises

Complete the following questions.

1. What famous tunes were sung during the Revolutionary and Civil Wars?

   _____

   _____

2. Which film focused on the first black army regiment in the Civil War?

   _____ Did you see this film? _____

*3. Which twentieth-century songwriter provided the music and words to

   Over There? _____ During which war was this

   song popular? _____

4. Which well-known patriotic song, made famous by singer Kate Smith, is

   regarded as a second national anthem in the United States?

   _____ Do you know this song? _____

5. How have the tragic events of September 11, 2001 influenced the

   popularity of this song? _____

   _____

6. Describe when and by whom the lyrics for *The Star-Spangled Banner* were

   written. _____

   _____

   _____

7. Which national anthems can be viewed as songs of war or independence?

   _____

   _____

8. Who wrote the *Emperor's Hymn,* which serves as the anthem of Austia?

   _____ Which other country has adopted

   this song? _____

9. What is the Canadian national anthem? _____

   Who wrote it, and when? _____

Activity

Watch a video from the library or a video store of the 1942 film classic *Yankee Doodle Dandy*, starring James Cagney as George M. Cohan. Note which songs from the show had inspirational or patriotic texts. Describe the setting of the film and its patriotic focus.

Or visit StudySpace (www.wwnorton.com/enjoy), read the Cultural Perspective, and follow   links provided there. Write an essay describing your online research.

---

83. *Listen* Still and Copland

*Still: *Afro-American Symphony,* Second Movement (**LG** 74, *e***LG**)
 Copland: *Street in a Frontier Town,* from *Billy the Kid* (**LG** 75, **Sh** 43, *e***LG**)

Exercises

Listen to *Street in a Frontier Town* from Copland's *Billy the Kid* while following the Listening Guide, then answer questions 1–7.

1. Briefly describe the story of *Billy the Kid.*_____

_____

_____

2. Suggest how each musical element below supports the story.

   Melody:_____

   Rhythm/meter: _____

   Harmony: _____

   Choice of instruments: _____

   _____

3. How does the composer evoke a Mexican dance?

   _____

   _____

4. Do you recognize any of the tunes Copland uses in this work? _____

   If yes, which? _____

5. Does he use the tunes literally? _____ Explain. _____

   _____

6. List two other ballets by Copland and tell how each is nationalistic.

   a. _____

   _____

   b. _____

   _____

7. How did Copland become familiar with American folk music?

   _____

   _____

   _____

*Listen to second movement of William Grant Still's *Afro-American Symphony* while following the Listening Guide, then answer questions 8–14.

8. What were Still's goals in composing the *Afro-American Symphony?*

_____

_____

9. On whose poetry are the symphony's movement loosely based?

_____

10. Describe which formal elements of the symphony are traditional.

_____

_____

11. Describe aspects of the symphony that depart from tradition.

_____

_____

12. Describe the nature of the first theme in the symphony's second movement. _____

_____

ABOUT THE COMPOSER

13. For which well-known TV series did Still write music?

_____

14. What other African-American composers and writers were influential to Still? _____

_____

84. *Listen* Revueltas and Mariachi Music
Revueltas: *Homenaje a Federico García Lorca*, Third Movement, *Son* (**LG** 76,
Sh 44, *e***LG**)
El Cihualteco (**LG** 77, Sh 45, *e***LG**)

Exercises

Listen to the third movement of Revueltas's *Homenaje a Federico García Lorca*,
while following the Listening Guide, then answer questions 1–10.

1. What Mexican folk ensemble is alluded to in *Homenaje a Federico García*

   Lorca? _____ How does Revueltas evoke this sound?

   _____

2. Who is Federico García Lorca and why did Revueltas wish to honor him?

   _____

   _____

3. What is unusual about the makeup of the orchestra for this work?

   _____

4. What is the meaning of the title of the third movement (*Son*)?

   _____

5. How would you characterize the treatment of rhythm and meter in this

   work? _____

   _____

6. What term best describes the overall form of this movement?

   _____

ABOUT THE COMPOSER AND HIS TIME

7. What is "mestizo realism"? _____

   _____

8. Who were some other influential Mexican composers of this era?

   _____

9. How was Revueltas's music viewed in his day? _____

   _____

10. What is Revueltas's best known orchestral work?_____

    What was the inspiration for this work? _____

   _____

167

Read Music from the Mariachi Tradition and listen to *El Cihualteco* while following the Listening Guide, then answer questions 11–21.

11. In which region of Mexico did the mariachi ensemble originate?

_____

12. What is a guitarrón? _____

    A vihuela?_____

13. Which mariachi group made over 200 movies?

_____

14. Describe the metric style of sesquialtera. _____

_____

_____

15. What is a *son*?_____

16. What does the title *El Cihualteco* mean? _____

17. What type of dance is associated with this *son*?_____

18. What is perhaps the most widely known mariachi dance?

_____

19. What meter do you hear most prominently in *El Cihualteco*?

_____

20. How many verses are sung in the *son*? _____ how many

    choruses? _____

21. What various kinds of dances do mariachi groups play today?

_____

_____

85. *Explore* Preserving the Musical Traditions of Mexico
CP 18

Exercises

Complete the following questions.

1. Which works by American composer Aaron Copland reflect his interest in Latin American music? _____

   _____

2. Which Latin American composer invited Copland to Mexico and when?

   _____

3. Which dance hall in Mexico City inspired a work by Copland?

   _____

4. What characteristics attracted Copland to the traditional music of Mexico? _____

5. What instruments are included in a traditional mariachi ensemble?

   _____

   _____

6. Who is a preeminent Mexican composer today? _____

7. List several of his works here and their literary bases:

   WORK   BASIS

   _____   _____

   _____   _____

   _____   _____

8. Describe this modern composer's style. _____

   _____

9. Name two important Mexican painters. _____

   _____

iMusic Listening Assignment (Student Resource Disc)

Listen again to *El Cihualteco* on your iMusic and describe below the instruments heard, the melodic and rhythmic style, the overall structure, and the singing.

Or visit StudySpace (www.wwnorton.com/enjoy), read the Cultural Perspective, and follow links provided there. Write an essay describing your online research.

86. *Review* Early Jazz Styles
Chap. 79, Sh 71

Exercises

Complete the following questions.

1. What styles merged to form early jazz? _____

   _____

2. What is ragtime? _____

   _____

   Who is considered the "king of ragtime"? _____

   What famous rags did he write? _____

   _____

3. What were his musical goals for ragtime? _____

   _____

4. In which classical genre did he compose? _____

   What is his most famous work in this genre? _____

   _____

5. What is the typical poetic form of a blues text?

   _____

   _____

6. Write one verse of your own that could be sung to the blues.

   _____

   _____

   _____

7. What is the standard musical form in blues? _____

   _____

8. What is a "blue note"? _____

9. Name a great female blues singer. _____

10. Which instruments would generally be heard in New Orleans jazz?

   _____

   _____

11. What is scat singing? _____

_____

Who is credited with inventing it? _____

True or False

____ 12. New Orleans-style jazz spread across the country in the 1920s.

____ 13. The clarinet was often featured in New Orleans jazz bands.

____ 14. Louis Armstrong was a noted jazz trombone player.

____ 15. Ella Fitzgerald was a virtuoso scat singer.

____ 16. Billie Holiday sang only with African-American performers.

____ 17. A vocable is a text syllable with no meaning.

18. Describe some of the difficulties Billie Holiday had throughout her life.

_____

_____

_____

87. *Explore* The Roots of Jazz
CP 19

Exercises

Complete the following questions.

1. From which cultures does jazz draw musical elements?

_____

_____

2. What singing styles still heard in certain African-American communities

have African origins? _____

_____

3. What is a work song? _____

_____

4. What is a spiritual? _____

_____

5. In which American city was jazz "born"? _____

6. What characterized nineteenth-century African-American music?

_____

_____

7. What is a griot? _____

_____

8. Describe performances in Congo Square in New Orleans.

_____

_____

_____

9. How did rural, or country, blues develop? Name a great singer in this

style. _____

_____

10. How did ragtime spread throughout the United States and Europe?

_____

_____

iMusic Listening Assignment (Student Resource Disc)

Listen to these three iMusic selections, representing precursors to jazz and early jazz styles, and describe aspects of the melody, rhythm, harmony, form, and instrumentation for each.

> *Swing Low, Sweet Chariot*
> Joplin: *Pine Apple Rag*
> *When the Saints Go Marching In*

Or visit StudySpace (www.wwnorton.com/enjoy), read the Cultural Perspective, and follow links provided there. Write an essay describing your online research.

---

88. *Listen* Ragtime, Blues, and Early Jazz
Joplin: *Maple Leaf Rag* (**LG** 78, Sh 46, *e***LG**)
Holiday: *Billie's Blues* (**LG** 79, Sh 47, *e***LG**)

Exercises

Listen to the recording of Scott Joplin playing his own *Maple Leaf Rag* while following the Listening Guide, then answer questions 1–6.

1. What stylistic element gives ragtime its name? _____

_____

2. What is a strain? _____

How long is each strain in *Maple Leaf Rag*? _____

3. Outline the form of the work. _____

Can you hear the repeated sections? _____

4. How did Joplin record this work? _____

_____

5. Which strain is heard in a new key (other than the tonic)? _____

6. What is the role of the left hand (bass part) in this piece? _____

_____

The right hand? _____

_____

Listen to *Billie's Blues* by Billie Holiday while following the Listening Guide, then answer questions 7–13.

7. What is the form of *Billie's Blues*? _____

8. Which chorus is a typical blues verse in terms of text structure?

_____

9. How many choruses are heard in this selection? _____

10. Which solo instruments can be heard in the fourth and fifth choruses

of *Billie's Blues*? _____

_____

11. What kind of pitch inflections are typical in the blues? _____

_____

12. How do each of the soloists (Holiday, Shaw, and Berrigan) contribute their own styles to this performance of *Billie's Blues?*

Holiday: _____

_____

Shaw: _____

_____

Berrigan: _____

_____

13. What jazz performers influenced Holiday as she developed her own style? _____

---

89. *Review* **The Swing Era and Later Jazz Styles**
Chap. 80, Sh 72

Exercises

Complete the following questions.

1. What decades are associated with the swing, or big band, era?

   _____

2. What was the economic situation in the United States during this era?

   _____

3. What jazz pianist/composer played a major role in the development of

   the swing era? _____

4. Name a musician/composer associated with each style listed below:

   bebop:_____

   cool jazz:_____

   West coast jazz:_____

   avant-garde jazz:_____

   free jazz: _____

5. What term refers to the merger of classical art music and jazz? _____

   Who is credited with this concept? _____

6. Which modern jazz trumpet player has exploited this style?

   _____

7. What is fusion? _____

   Name some fusion artists. _____

   _____

8. Name two American composers who have successfully merged classical

   and jazz styles in their compositions. _____

   _____

9. Describe the character of Gershwin's songs. _____

   _____

10. How do his songs differ from his instrumental works? _____

    _____

11. What is Gershwin's most famous work?

_____

12. When was it premiered and by whom? _____

_____

13. How have new technologies affected the composition and performance
    of jazz? _____

_____

_____

90. *Listen* Big Band, Bebop, and Beyond
*Strayhorn/Ellington: *Take the A Train* (**LG** 80, *e***LG**)
  Gillespie/Parker: *A Night in Tunisia* (**LG** 81, Sh 48, *e***LG**)
*Gershwin: Piano Prelude No. 1 (**LG** 82, *e***LG**)

Exercises

*Listen to *Take the A Train* by Strayhorn/Ellington while following the Listening Guide, then answer questions 1–6.

1. What is the form of *Take the A Train?* _____

2. What is the medium? _____

3. What solo instruments are featured in *Take the A Train?*

   _____

   Who are the soloists on this recording? _____

   _____

4. How is "call and response" used in this piece? _____

   _____

5. What effects can be heard in the trumpet solo? _____

   _____

6. What makes assigning the authorship of this piece to Strayhorn or

   Ellington difficult? _____

   _____

Listen to *A Night in Tunisia* by Gillespie/Parker while following the Listening Guide, then answer questions 7–13.

7. Which two jazz legends are featured in our recording of *A Night in*

   Tunisia? _____

   What instruments do they play? _____

8. Who composed the tune? _____

   What does he play? _____

9. What size ensemble plays this jazz selection? _____

10. In bebop and other jazz styles, the tune is presented first, followed by:

   _____

11. What is a break, and where does one occur in *A Night in Tunisia?*

_____

_____

12. What is a jazz riff? _____

_____

13. How would you describe Parker's style of improvisation? _____

_____

*Listen to Gershwin's Piano Prelude No. 1 while following the Listening Guide, then answer questions 14–17.

14. What is the form of Gershwin's Piano Prelude No. 1? _____

15. What does "Allegro ben ritmato e deciso" mean? _____

_____

16. What jazz elements can be heard in Piano Prelude No. 1? _____

_____

17. What other instrumental works by Gershwin combine elements of jazz with classical forms? _____

_____

91. *Review* American Musical Theater
Chap. 81, Sh 73

Exercises

Fill in the information below.

1. Out of which European stage genre did musical theater develop?

   _____

2. Name a popular musical from the 1920s: _____

   from the 1930s: _____

   from the 1940s: _____

   from the 1950s: _____

3. List three musicals with a literary basis and name the source for each.

   MUSICAL   BASIS

   _____   _____

   _____   _____

   _____   _____

4. Name two famous Broadway musical composer/lyricist teams and a show by each.

   COMPOSER/LYRICIST   SHOW

   _____   _____

   _____   _____

Match the following well-known musicals with their writers.

____ 5. *Into the Woods*   a. Stephen Sondheim

____ 6. *Les Misérables*   b. Andrew Lloyd Webber

____ 7. *Evita*   c. Claude-Michel Schonberg

____ 8. *Jesus Christ Superstar*

____ 9. *Cats*

____ 10. *Phantom of the Opera*

____ 11. *Miss Saigon*

____ 12. *Sweeney Todd*

13. Name several classical musicals that have recently been revived on Broadway. _____

14. Name a musical that has a tragic ending. _____

15. Name a classic musical that deals with African-American life and uses folk elements. _____

16. When was the first rock musical written? _____

What was it? _____

What are some others? _____

_____

17. Name two new musicals produced by the Disney studio.

_____

18. What is the basis for each of the two recent shows listed below?

a. *Ragtime*: _____

b. *Rent*: _____

19. List several shows that you have seen (on stage or on video). Give the composer and lyricist.

a. _____

b. _____

c. _____

20. Recent musicals have been written on such literary classics as *Les Misérables* and *The Phantom of the Opera*. Suggest a book that you think could be adapted for the musical theater stage, and tell why you believe it could succeed.

_____

_____

_____

_____

_____

_____

92. *Listen* Bernstein's *West Side Story*
Bernstein: *West Side Story*, excerpts (**LG** 83, Sh 49, *e***LG**)

Exercises

Listen to excerpts from Bernstein's *West Side Story* while following the
Listening Guide, then answer the questions below.

1. Who wrote the lyrics to *West Side Story?* _____

2. What is the story about? _____

   _____

   On what is it based? _____

3. What gives the Mambo in *West Side Story* its Latin-American flavor?

   _____

   What gives it a jazz-like character? _____

   _____

4. What is the structure of the ballad *Tonight?* _____

   Can you hear the sections? _____

5. How is the *Tonight* ensemble like an operatic ensemble number?

   _____

   _____

   _____

6. How are the music and story of *West Side Story* still relevant today?

   _____

   _____

   _____

ABOUT THE COMPOSER

7. Is Bernstein a classical or a popular composer? Explain your response.

   _____

   _____

   _____

8. In addition to composing, what other musical roles did Bernstein fill during his lifetime? _____

_____

_____

9. How did Bernstein first receive recognition as a conductor?

_____

_____

_____

---

93. *Explore* Latin American Dance Music
CP 20

Exercises

Complete the following questions.

*1. Name several Latin-American dances that have become popular in Europe and America, and identify their countries of origin.

_____

_____

_____

2. What are the two meanings of the word "conga"? _____

_____

_____

3. To what musical style does the term "salsa" refer? _____

_____

_____

4. When does the festival of Carnival occur? _____

5. When is it celebrated in the Republic of Trinidad and Tobago?

_____

6. What season in the church year marks the end of Carnival? _____

7. What are steel drums made from? _____

8. How are steel drums tuned? _____

_____

9. Where did ska and reggae originate? _____

Describe the musical style of ska. _____

_____

_____

Which pop song introduced the style into the United States?

_____

10. Describe the musical characteristics of reggae. _____

_____

11. Name several well-known reggae artists. _____

_____

185

iMusic Listening Assignment (Student Resource Disc)

Listen to the *Dougla Dance* excerpt in the iMusic recordings and describe the rhythmic character of the dance, its form, and the timbre heard in the instruments. Describe how steel drums are made to produce this timbre.

Or visit StudySpace (www.wwnorton.com/enjoy), read the Cultural Perspective, and follow links provided there. Write an essay describing your online research.

_____

_____

_____

_____

_____

_____

_____

_____

_____

_____

_____

_____

_____

_____

_____

_____

_____

_____

_____

_____

_____

_____

_____

_____

_____

_____

94. *Review* A History of Rock
Chap. 82, Sh 74

Exercises

Complete the following questions.

1. What is rhythm and blues? _____

   Name several performers of this style. _____

   _____

2. What other styles of music contributed to the development of rock and

   roll? _____

3. Name two African-American and two white rock-and-roll stars from the
   1950s.

   African American: _____

   White: _____

4. Describe briefly each of the following popular styles, and name at least
   one performer or group associated with each.

   a. Soft rock: _____

      Group: _____

   b. Acid rock: _____

      Group: _____

   c. Art rock: _____

      Group: _____

   d. Heavy metal: _____

      Group: _____

   e. Punk rock: _____

      Group: _____

   f. Reggae: _____

      Group: _____

   g. Rap: _____

      Group: _____

   h. Grunge rock: _____

      Group: _____

5. Why are the Beatles so important to the history of rock? _____

_____

What accounts for their continued popularity? _____

_____

6. How did rock videos and MTV change the way people listen to and judge popular music? _____

_____

7. What other technological developments have revolutionized rock?

_____

_____

8. What two groups or performers from the 1980s do you think were the most influential to the development of rock? _____

_____

9. What "classic" rock groups have had successful revivals? _____

_____

_____

10. What groups that are currently popular do you think will be remembered ten years from now? _____

_____

_____

11. How has the role of women in popular music changed recently?

_____

_____

12. Where did country/western music originate? _____

_____

13. What instruments are typically found in bluegrass? _____

_____

14. Name several "classic" country/western performers. _____

_____

15. Name several musicians currently popular on the country/western scene:

_____

---

95. *Listen* The Global Scene

BeauSoleil: *Think of Me* (**LG** 84, Sh 50, *e***LG**)
*Ladysmith Black Mambazo: *Homeless* (**LG** 85, *e***LG**)

Exercises

Listen to the BeauSoleil performance of the Cajun dance *Think of Me* while following the Listening Guide, then answer questions 1–6.

1. In what part of the United States did Cajun music originate?

   _____ What are the cultural roots of the

   Cajuns? _____

2. What instruments are typically heard in Cajun dance music?

   _____

   _____

3. What are some of the special effects heard in this recording?

   _____

   _____

4. What term best describes the texture of *Think of Me?*

   _____

5. In which language is the text of *Think of Me?* _____

6. What musical characteristics give this dance a sense of regularity?

   _____

   What makes it complex? _____

   _____

*Listen to the Ladysmith Black Mambazo performance of *Homeless* while following the Listening Guide, then answer questions 7–13.

7. What type of ensemble is this? _____

   Who is the leader? _____

8. Describe the singing style heard in this song. _____

   _____

   _____

9. What elements of this style have traditional African roots?

_____

_____

   Which African culture developed this style? _____

10. What sounds Western about this song? _____

_____

11. For what historic albun was *Homeless* written?

_____

12. How did Paul Simon help promote the music of South Africa?

_____

_____

13. What modern U.S. disaster echoes the theme of *Homeless*?

_____

96. *Review* The New Music
Chaps. 83–84, Sh 75–76

Exercises

Complete the following questions.

1. Name an artist associated with each of the following trends.

   a. Pop Art: _____

   b. Post-Modernism: _____

   c. Abstract Expressionism: _____

   d. New wave cinema: _____

   e. Performance art: _____

   f. Feminist art: _____

   g. Ethnic art: _____

2. List one or more major figures of the second half of the twentieth century in each discipline below and cite a work by each.

   a. Poem: _____

   _____

   b. Stage work: _____

   _____

   c. Novel: _____

   _____

   d. Film: _____

   _____

True or False

____ 3. Total serialism is an extension of twelve-tone music to include the complex organization of other musical elements.

____ 4. Aleatoric music refers to an ultrarational, total serial music.

____ 5. Open form is a flexible structure related to aleatoric music.

____ 6. John Cage was associated with aleatoric music.

____ 7. The piano is not capable of playing microtones, because they fall between its keys.

____ 8. Western composers have been influenced by the tuning systems and instruments of various Asian cultures.

Match the following contemporary composers with their native countries. You may use an answer more than once.

_____ 9. Pierre Boulez   a. Poland

_____ 10. Luciano Berio   b. Russia

_____ 11. Milton Babbitt   c. Hungary

_____ 12. Krzysztof Penderecki   d. France

_____ 13. Karlheinz Stockhausen   e. Italy

_____ 14. Sofia Gubaidulina   f. Germany

_____ 15. John Cage   g. United States

_____ 16. George Crumb

17. Name two female virtuoso singers who have specialized in contemporary music. _____

_____

18. What unusual techniques have they specialized in? _____

_____

_____

19. The roles of women in music, especially as composers, have changed radically over the centuries. What general perception do you have of the roles of women in classical music today?

_____

_____

_____

_____

_____

97. *Explore* Public Support for New Music
CP 21

Exercises

Complete the following questions.

1. What is IRCAM and how has it contributed to the composition of new music? _____

_____

_____

2. When and by whom was IRCAM formed? _____

_____

3. Which composer was appointed to lead this center?

_____

4. Name several important music institutions in Canada.

_____

_____

5. Which composer is often considered the "father of contemporary Canadian music"? _____

6. Which Canadian organization provides information about new music in Canada? _____

7. In 1970, Canada took the bold step to require AM radio stations to include a particular percentage of Canadian music. What was the percentage?

_____

8. Which living composer is perhaps Canada's best known?

_____

Name one of his works: _____

9. How does support for the arts in the U.S. measure up against that in Canada and France? _____

_____

10. How important do you think it is to have government support of the artistic and cultural heritage of your country? _____

_____

Listening Assignment

Investigate a multimedia or performance art work by one of the composers listed below. Read about the work, listen to it (if possible), and discuss how it changes standard conventions of performance.

> Laurie Anderson
> John Cage
> Pauline Oliveros
> R. Murray Schafer

Or visit StudySpace (www.wwnorton.com/enjoy), read the Cultural Perspective, and follow links provided there. Write an essay describing your online research.

Work: _____ Date: _____

Composer: _____

Medium (performance forces): _____

_____

Description of work: _____

_____

_____

_____

_____

_____

How does a performance of this work differ from standard performance rituals?

_____

_____

_____

_____

_____

_____

Comments: _____

_____

_____

_____

_____

_____

---

98. *Listen* The New Virtuosity: Messiaen, Boulez, and Crumb
*Messiaen: *Vocalise* from *Quartet for the End of Time* (**LG** 86, *e***LG**)
*Boulez: *Notations IV* (**LG** 87, *e***LG**)
 Crumb: *Ancient Voices of Children*, First Movement (**LG** 88, Sh 51, *e***LG**)

Exercises

*Listen to the *Vocalise* from Messiaen's *Quartet for the End of Time* while following the Listening Guide, then answer questions 1–5.

  1. Where and under what circumstances was this work written?

_____

  2. What is its instrumentation? _____

      Where was it premiered? _____

  3. What biblical passage inspired this quartet? _____

      What is the passage about? _____

_____

  4. In the *Vocalise, for the Angel who announces the End of Time,* how do the

      music at the opening and closing evoke the program? _____

_____

      What makes the middle section sound angelic? _____

_____

  5. What are some of the influences on Messiaen's music other than the

      circumstances surrounding the *Quartet for the End of Time?* _____

_____

*Listen to Boulez's *Notations IV* for orchestra while following the Listening Guide, then answer questions 6–13.

  6. For which medium did Boulez originally write *Notations?* _____

      When did he write this first version? _____

  7. What is unusual about the orchestra for this work? _____

_____

  8. What is a hexachord? _____

      How many different hexachords does Boulez use in this movement?

_____

9. Describe the interrelationship between the hexachords and their pitches.

_____

_____

10. Describe Boulez's use of ostinato in this work. _____

_____

11. How would you describe the level of dissonance? _____

_____

12. How do you think the general concert-going public reacts on first

hearing a work like this? _____

_____

13. What important musical positions has Pierre Boulez held?

_____

_____

Listen to *The Little Boy Is Looking for His Voice* from Crumb's *Ancient Voices of Children* while following the Listening Guide, then answer questions 14–22.

14. Whose poetry is set in this song cycle? _____

15. What other works did Crumb set to texts by the same poet?

_____

16. What is unusual about the instruments used in this work?

_____

17. What unusual effects is the voice asked to reproduce?

_____

18. Describe the vocalise singing style that opens this song.

_____

_____

19. Can you hear when the text is finally sung? _____

20. Who sings the second strophe of the song? _____

What is unusual about the way this is sung? _____

_____

21. What non-Western styles are suggested in this song? _____

_____

22. What extraordinary singer recorded this work? _____

---

99. *Listen* The Influence of World Music: Cage, Ligeti, and Sheng

Cage: Sonata V, from *Sonatas and Interludes* (**LG** 89, Sh 52, *e***LG**)
*Ligeti: *Disorder*, from *Etudes for Piano*, Book I (**LG** 91, *e***LG**)
Sheng: *China Dreams: Prelude* (**LG** 93, Sh 54, *e***LG**)

Exercises

Listen to Cage's Sonata V from *Sonatas and Interludes* while following the Listening Guide, then answer questions 1–5.

1. What is the overall structure of Cage's *Sonatas and Interludes?*

   _____

   _____

2. What is the form of Sonata V? _____

3. What is a prepared piano? _____

   _____

4. What musical influence led Cage to develop the prepared piano?

   _____

   _____

5. Describe the timbre in your own words. _____

   _____

   _____

*Listen to *Disorder* from Ligeti's *Etudes for Piano*, Book I, while following the Listening Guide, then answer questions 6–12.

6. What influenced Ligeti's writing in these études?

   _____

   _____

7. What element is manipulated the most in this work? _____

8. Why is the title *Disorder* appropriate for this work?

   _____

   _____

9. How would you describe the character of this piano work?

   _____

10. How does the étude end? _____

_____

11. How demanding do you think this work is to perform?

_____

12. What famous film made use of Ligeti's music? _____

What works were included in this soundtrack? _____

_____

Have you seen this film? _____

When was it made? _____

Who was the film's director? _____

Listen to the *Prelude* from Bright Sheng's *China Dreams* while following the Listening Guide, then answer questions 13–17.

13. What genre best describes *China Dreams*? _____

14. How is the work programmatic? _____

_____

15. What Asian qualities can be heard in this work? _____

_____

16. What Western qualities do you hear? _____

_____

17. What other works did Bright Sheng write that evoke his homeland?

_____

_____

---

100. *Listen* **World Music: The Sounds of Java and Eastern Africa**
Javanese Gamelan Music: *Patalon* (**LG** 90, Sh 53, *e***LG**)
*East African Music: *Ensiraba ya munange Katego* (**LG** 92, *e***LG**)

Exercises

Listen to *Patalon* while following the Listening Guide, then answer questions 1–6.

1. What is a gamelan? _____

_____

In which cultures is this ensemble used? _____

For what types of events is it used? _____

2. What is the story told in the play from which the *Patalon* comes?

_____

_____

_____

What is the basis for this story? _____

3. What function does the *Patalon* play for the entire drama? _____

_____

4. What type of scale is featured in this work? _____

5. Describe what distinguishes the different sections of the work.

_____

_____

Can you hear the distinct sections and changes in timbre? _____

6. Of the composers we studied, which was (were) particularly influenced by the sound of the gamelan?

_____

*Listen to the selection of Ugandan drumming, *Ensiraba ya munange Katego*, while following the Listening Guide, then answer questions 7–17.

7. Name an instrument in each category below that is played in Eastern

Africa.

Chordophone: _____

Idiophone: _____

199

Aerophone: _____

Membranophone: _____

8. What is an entenga ensemble? _____

9. How many players participate? _____ On how many drums? _____

10. How many drums (and pitches) does each melody drummer play? _____

11. What is the story told by this piece? _____

_____

_____

12. When the players begin, only rhythmic clicking is heard. Why?

_____

_____

13. How many different rhythmic patterns are actually played? _____

14. Can you hear the interlocking patterns and resulting complexity once
    the drummers move their strokes to the drum heads? _____

15. How did entenga players learn their parts in such a piece?

_____

_____

16. Which contemporary composer that we studied was influenced by this
    style of music? _____

17. Can you hear any relationship between this African drumming selection
    and the piano étude *Disorder*? _____

iMusic Listening (Student Resource Disc)

Gota

18. What African singing technique is heard at the beginning of this excerpt?
    ____ polytextuality ____ call and response ____ vocal glides

19. Check all categories of world instruments heard in this excerpt (aside
    from voice): ____ idiophones ____ aerophones ____ chordophones
    ____ membranophones

20. How would you describe the rhythmic treatment in this excerpt from
    Ghana? _____

101. *Listen* World Music: Chinese Traditional Music
Abing: *The Moon Reflected on the Second Springs* (**LG** 94, Sh 55, *e***LG**)

Exercises

Listen to the traditional Chinese selection *The Moon Reflected on the Second Springs* while following the Listening Guide, then answer the questions below.

1. Which Chinese musician composed and first performed this work?

   _____

2. Which region of China is he from? _____

3. Describe this musician's life. _____

   _____

   _____

   _____

4. The musician was a Daoist; what does this mean?

   _____

5. Why do we consider this "composed" work traditional music?

   _____

   _____

6. For what instrument was *The Moon Reflected on the Second Springs*

   conceived? _____ Describe the instrument.

   _____

7. What additional instrument is heard on our recording?

   _____ Describe this instrument.

   _____

8. What type of scale is this work based on? _____

9. What are the pitches? _____

10. How many phrases make up the melody of this work? _____

    Are they symmetrical in length? _____

11. What does "jia hua" mean? _____

How does the technique sound musically? _____

_____

12. How many times is the complete melody played? _____

Can you hear when it repeats? _____

13. Describe the sound of the erhu in your own words. Compare it with

the Western violin. _____

_____

_____

_____

_____

_____

14. Describe how the yangqin sounds and the role it serves in this

performance. _____

_____

_____

_____

iMusic Listening (Student Resource Disc)

In a Mountain Path

15. This Chinese example features erhu and yangqin. Describe what makes
it sound foreign (non-Western). Consider the melody, texture, and
playing style.

_____

_____

_____

_____

_____

_____

102. *Explore* Improvisation as Compositional Process
CP 22

Exercises

Complete the following questions.

1. Define improvisation in music._____

_____

_____

2. What are the roles of the composer and performer in an improvised

   composition? _____

_____

3. Is the Chinese work *The Moon Reflected on the Second Springs* entirely

   improvised? _____

4. Who first "composed" this work? _____

5. What kind of "rules" does a raga present in the classical music of India?

_____

*6. What are the sections of a classical Indian work?

_____

7. What instruments are traditionally involved in a North Indian classical

   performance? _____

_____

*8. What is the term in Iranian music for short melodic building blocks?

_____

9. Are the scales the same in Iranian music as in Western music?

   _____ Explain. _____

_____

_____

10. What kind of ornamental or decorative notes are used in Iranian music?

_____

iMusic Listening Assignment (Student Resource Disc)

Listen to the Iranian piece *Avaz of Bayate Esfahan* from the iMusic selections and describe how the melodic ideas grow and are decorated. Consider how rhythm and harmony are used in this style as well.

Or visit StudySpace (www.wwnorton.com/enjoy), read the Cultural Perspective, and follow links provided there. Write an essay describing your online research.

---

103. *Review* Music for Films
Chap. 86, Sh 78

Exercises

Complete the following questions.

1. Describe an example in which music establishes the mood in a film.

   _____

   _____

2. Describe an example in which music helps establish a character.

   _____

3. Describe how music can help give a sense of place and time in a film.

   _____

4. What does "running counter to the action" mean? _____

   _____

5. What is the difference between "underscoring" and "source music"?

   _____

   _____

   _____

6. What is a leitmotif? _____

   Name a film in which a leitmotif is integral to the soundtrack.

   _____

7. How was music provided for silent films?_____

   _____

8. What was the first "talkie," or film with a soundtrack?

   _____

   When was it issued? _____

9. Name a film for which each of these composers wrote the music.

   a. Max Steiner: _____

   b. Erich Wolfgang Korngold: _____

   c. Bernard Herrmann: _____

   d. Miklós Rózsa:_____

   Do you know any of these films? _____

10. What were Prokofiev's two great epic film scores?

_____

_____

11. Name an American art music composer who also wrote music for several Oscar-nominated films. _____

12. Which films with music by John Williams have you seen?

_____

_____

With music by James Horner? _____

_____

13. Name a popular film with music by Danny Elfman.

_____

With music by Hans Zimmer: _____

14. Do you feel that any of the above composers has a recognizable style?

_____ Explain. _____

_____

_____

Match the following composers with their film scores.

_____ 15. Elmer Bernstein   a. *Crouching Tiger, Hidden Dragon*

_____ 16. Jerry Goldsmith   b. *The Truman Show*

_____ 17. Rachel Portman   c. *The Red Violin*

_____ 18. Philip Glass   d. *The Cider House Rules*

_____ 19. John Corigliano   e. *Planet of the Apes*

_____ 20. Tan Dun   f. *Wild Wild West*

Which of these films have you seen? _____

_____

---

104. *Listen* **Film Composers Sergei Prokofiev and John Williams**
*Prokofiev: *Alexander Nevsky*, Seventh Movement (**LG** 95, *e***LG**)
John Williams: *Raiders March,* from *Raiders of the Lost Ark* (**LG** 96, Sh 56, *e***LG**)

Exercises

*Listen to the excerpt from *Alexander Nevsky* while following the Listening Guide, then answer questions 1–8.

1. What is the basis for the story of *Alexander Nevsky?*

_____

2. Who directed the film for which this music was originally written?

_____ When was the film made?

_____ When was this music reworked into a cantata?

_____

3. How did the film *Alexander Nevsky* and its music serve to bolster the

morale of the Russians? _____

_____

4. What aspects of the last movement of the cantata *Alexander Nevsky*

sound particularly Russian? _____

_____

Can you follow the Russian text in the Listening Guide? _____

ABOUT THE COMPOSER

5. What political pressures did Prokofiev experience in his career?

_____

_____

6. What elements of Classicism are heard in Prokofiev's music?

_____

7. How did he strive for innovation? _____

_____

8. Name several well-known works by Prokofiev. _____

_____

Listen to John Williams's *Raiders March* from *Raiders of the Lost Ark* while following the Listening Guide, then answer questions 9–14.

9. In what year was this film released? _____

10. What are the two leitmotifs heard in this excerpt? _____

_____

Who do they represent? _____

_____

11. What is the overall form of the march? _____

12. How does the instrumentation support the marchlike character of the work? _____

13. What is the melodic character of the opening march melody?

_____

14. What is the more lyrical section of a march called?

_____

---

105. *Review* Technology and Music
Chap. 87, Sh 79
Tod Machover: *Begin Again Again . . .* from *Hyperstring Trilogy* (**LG** 97, Sh 57, *e***LG**)

Exercises

Complete the following questions.

1. What is *musique concrète?* _____

   When and where did it emerge? _____

   *Name several composers associated with this trend. _____

   _____

2. How did the German *electronische Musik* differ from *musique concrète?*

   _____

3. What are some ways that composers manipulated tape in the early days

   of electronic music? _____

   _____

4. Name an electronic music work by the German composer Karlheinz

   Stockhausen. _____

5. What device was at the heart of the German electronic music studio?

   _____ What did it do? _____

   How was it important to later developments in electronic music?

   _____

6. The _____ was the first completely integrated

   music synthesizer. Why did so few composers have a chance to use it?

   _____

7. Who is credited with the creation of compact, affordable synthesizers?

   _____

8. Which best-selling synthesizer employed FM synthesis technology

   (brand new at the time)? _____

9. What is MIDI? _____

   _____

10. How did the development of digital sampling synthesizers advance musical composition? _____

_____

Match the composers with their descriptions.

_____ 11. Edgard Varèse   a. composed *Poème électronique* for a sound and light show at the World's Fair in Brussels

_____ 12. Mario Davidovsky   b. composer/creator of the interactive installation *Brain Opera*

_____ 13. Milton Babbit   c. wrote works for tape and live performer, such as *Synchronisms*

_____ 14. Tod Machover   d. composed *Philomel* and *Philonema* at the Columbia-Princeton Electronic Music Center

Listen to the excerpt from Machover's *Hyperstring Triology, Begin Again Again . . .* while following the Listening Guide, then answer questions 15–20.

15. What is a hyperinstrument? _____

_____

16. For which famous cellist did the composer write this work?

_____

17. Which literary epic inspired the composition of this work?

_____

18. Which Baroque composition is referred to in *Begin Again Again . . .* ?

_____

19. What are some of the different moods the composer tries to convey (given in the titles of the work's sections)? _____

_____

20. What is your reaction to this piece? _____

_____

_____

---

106. *Explore* **Musical Interactivity**
CP 23

Exercises

Complete the following questions.

*1. Which classic science fiction movie featured a singing computer?

_____

What song did the computer sing?_____

At what point during the film did this occur? _____

_____

2. Who is considered the father of computer music?

_____

3. How did Tod Machover's experiements engage the conductor in

interactive music-making? _____

_____

4. What is the derivation of the title *Bug-mudra*? _____

_____

5. How does Machover's *Brain Opera* involve the audience in the creative

process? _____

_____

6. Where is this work now permanently installed? _____

7. How has IRCAM encouraged young musicians to engage in interactive

creative endeavors? _____

_____

_____

Essay

Locate a recording of a work by Tod Machover (check your library or purchase one online). Describe some of the effects heard and how electronics have enhanced the music.

Or visit StudySpace (www.wwnorton.com/enjoy), read the Cultural Perspective, and follow links provided there. Write an essay describing your online research.

---

107. *Review* New Romanticism and Minimalism
Chap. 88, Sh 80

Exercises

Multiple Choice

____ 1. Which of the following best sums up the aspirations of composers
of the New Romanticism?
   a. purely intellectual, completely serial composition
   b. music as "the language of the emotions"
   c. formal, constructivist art

____ 2. The New Romantics sought to:
   a. close the gap between composers and listeners.
   b. further widen the gap between composers and listeners.
   c. follow the harmonic and melodic language of the Baroque.

Complete the following questions.

3. Which composer and work might be considered a precursor of the

   New Romanticism? _____

   _____

4. Why do you think this style has been especially popular with women

   composers? _____

   _____

   _____

Multiple Choice

____ 5. Which term best describes the marked stylistic feature of
minimalist music?
   a. dissonance
   b. repetition
   c. contrast

____ 6. What was the primary impetus for minimalist composers?
   a. a return to simplicity
   b. a total abandonment of form
   c. a desire for overstatement

7. Name three composers who are considered minimalists. _____

   _____

   _____

8. How would you describe the effect that minimalist music has on the listener? _____

_____

9. Name two operas by John Adams and the historical event that spawned each. _____

_____

10. Which style do you think will last longer: New Romanticism or minimalism? _____ Why? _____

_____

_____

11. What is spiritual minimalism? _____

_____

Name two composers who are considered spiritual minimalists.

_____

_____

12. During which famous historical event of 1997 was a spiritual minimalist work featured? _____

Which work? _____

> ### 108. *Listen* Today's Composers: Pärt, Adams, and Larsen
> Pärt: *Cantate Domino canticum novum* (**LG** 98, Sh 58, *e***LG**)
> Adams *Tromba lontana* (**LG** 99, Sh 59, *e***LG**)
> Larsen: *Sonnets from the Portuguese,* Nos. 5 and 6 (**LG** 100, Sh 60, *e***LG**)

Exercises

Listen to Arvo Pärt's *Cantate Domino canticum novum* while following the Listening Guide, then answer questions 1–6.

1. Where was the composer Arvo Pärt born? _____

2. How have the composer's religious beliefs influenced his compositions?

    _____

    _____

3. What is the source of the text for *Cantate Domino?* _____

    In what language is it sung? _____

4. How would you describe the texture of this work? _____

    _____

5. How does Pärt achieve the unique tintinnabular style in this work?

    _____

    _____

6. Can this work, and Pärt's style in general, be viewed as minimalist? _____

    If so, how? _____

    _____

Listen to the third movement of John Adams's *Tromba lontana* while following the Listening Guide, then answer questions 7–12.

7. For which orchestra and occasion was this work written? _____

    _____

8. Adams considered this work a fanfare. How can it be viewed as such?

    _____

9. How are the solo instruments placed in this work? _____

    _____

10. Describe how these solo instruments interact. _____

    _____

11. What instruments are used to achieve the bell-like timbre in the work?

_____

12. What are the minimalist characteristics in this work? _____

_____

Listen to Libby Larsen's two songs from *Sonnets from the Portuguese* while following the Listening Guide, then answer questions 13–20.

13. What are some of the texts by women that Libby Larsen has set to music?

_____

_____

14. Who wrote the poems set in the song cycle *Sonnets from the Portuguese?*

_____

15. When did this poet live? _____

16. Which well-known soprano worked with Larsen on these songs and first recorded them? _____

17. How would you describe the metric treatment in "Oh, Yes!"?

_____

18. What is a Musselman? _____
    a Giaour? _____

19. How would you describe the metric treatment in "How do I love thee?"?

_____

20. What is "Romantic" about these songs? (Consider their texts, melodies, and harmonies.) _____

_____

_____

_____

> **109.** *Review* **Music Notation**
> Appendix I

Exercises

Answer the following questions about the Minuet in D minor (from the
Anna Magdalena Notebook). The notation appears below and you can listen to
this in the iMusic examples.

1. Which two clef signs does this keyboard work use?

   _____ for the right hand; _____ for the left hand

2. The first pitch in the right hand is _____; this is sounded

   simultaneously with the first pitch in the left hand, which is _____.

3. The time signature indicates a triple meter (3/4). This means that a

   _____ note gets one beat, with _____ beats per measure.

4. How many eighth notes does it take to complete one measure? _____

   Which measure features this rhythmic treatment? _____

5. Would you consider this melody to be _____ conjunct or _____ disjunct?

6. The key signature at the beginning of the piece indicates a special

   symbol (♭) on the third line. What is this symbol called? _____

   What pitch does it change? _____ How does it change

   the pitch? _____

7. What is the sign (♯) next to the first note in measure 3? _____

   What is the pitch it changes? _____ How does it change

   the pitch? _____

8. At the end of measure 4, both hands play the same pitch. What is it? _____ What is it called when the pitches are the same but are in a different register? _____

9. In this meter, how many eighth notes make up one beat? _____

10. What is the meaning of the 1 and 2 with brackets over the music at the end of this example? _____

_____

11. Does this dance begin on an ____ upbeat or a ____ downbeat?

12. Which beat in each measure is the most accented? _____

13. In measure 7, a new rhythmic value is introduced. What is it?

_____

14. Does this piece have harmony? _____

15. Which best describes the texture? ____ homophonic or ____ polyphonic

16. Which line predominates? _____

17. What instrument is heard playing this piece? _____

18. Name a song you know that begins with an upbeat.

_____

19. Name a song you know that is in duple meter.

_____

20. What is the most common compound meter? _____

Name a song you know that is in a compound meter.

_____

21. Write a melody on the staff below, beginning with a clef, time signature, and key signature. You can make up the pitches and rhythms, but make sure your rhythmic notation is correct for each measure.

MUSIC ACTIVITIES

The following exercises allow you to explore various types of music on your own or with a small group (a study or discussion group, for example). They are designed to make you more aware of the diverse opportunities you have to hear music and to participate actively in making music. These exercises are meant to guide you in doing special projects and in completing work assigned by your instructor. The activities can be varied, and there are many possible variaions that could be educational. If you have ideas for projects, talk them over with your instructor.

Activity 1: Keep a Music Journal

Goal: To become more aware of music in your environment.

For four days, keep a journal in the space below, noting all the instances in which you listen to or hear music, whether by your own choosing or by accident. Consider the following in your journal: alarm clocks, car and/or home stereos, televisions (even as background music), work environments, classes, stores, and elevators.

Day 1: Date _____

AM: _____

_____

_____

_____

PM: _____

_____

_____

_____

_____

Day 2: Date _____

AM: _____

_____

_____

_____

PM: _____

_____

_____

_____

_____

Day 3: Date _____

AM: _____

_____

_____

_____

PM: _____

_____

_____

_____

_____

Day 4: Date _____

AM: _____

_____

_____

PM: _____

_____

_____

_____

_____

Were you surprised how often (or seldom) you heard music?

_____

Were you more aware than usual of music in your environment? _____

Was any of the music distracting or annoying? _____

Comments: _____

_____

_____

_____

_____

Activity 2: Interview a Musician

Goal: To gain insight into musical performance from an active participant.

Find a musician—performer or conductor—on campus (a music student or an instructor) and arrange an interview. Ask the musician the questions below, along with others that you supply.

Interview Questions

What is your name? _____

Are you ____ a performer, ____ a conductor, or ____ both?

How long have you studied music? _____

What instrument(s) do you play? _____

Do you sing? _____ If so, what voice range? _____

In which music ensembles have you participated and in what capacity?

_____

_____

_____

Do you take part in concerts frequently? _____

Approximately how many performances a year? _____

Describe a recent performance in which you participated (group, which instrument/voice, and repertory performed).

_____

_____

_____

_____

_____

How is active participation in music-making different from passive listening?

_____

_____

_____

_____

What decisions must you make while performing music?

_____

_____

_____

_____

What styles of music do you most often perform?

____ classical   ____ popular   ____ traditional

Describe the specific styles you perform frequently.

_____

_____

Do you now (or do you plan to) make your living as a musician?

____ yes ____ no

Comments: _____

What are the advantages of a career in music? _____

_____

_____

What are the disadvantages? _____

_____

_____

(Your comments here): _____

_____

_____

_____

_____

Activity 3: Interview an International Student

Goal: To learn about the music of another culture from a native of the culture.

Find an international student or instructor on your campus. (Ask in your classes, post a note on a student union or online bulletin board, or ask at the International Office on your campus.) Arrange to meet with this person and ask the questions below, along with others that you supply.

Interview Questions

What is your name? _____

What country do you come from? _____

What is your native language? _____

How long have you been in this country? _____

What are you studying here? _____

Have you ever studied music? _____

Do you play any instruments? _____ If so, which one(s)?

_____

Did you learn any native folk songs as a child? _____

Can you sing or play one, or tell me about one?

Title: _____ Language: _____

What is it about? _____

_____

_____

(To the interviewer: make your own notes about the song below.)

_____

_____

What kind of instruments are used in your native folk music?

_____

What roles does music play in your society? _____

_____

Do men and women study music in the same ways there? What kind of music? _____

_____

What kind of music do you like to listen to? _____

_____

Do you plan to take any music classes while studying here? _____
If so, which? _____
Have you been to any concerts in this country? _____
If so, which? _____

_____

Is popular music in your country influenced by American popular styles?
_____ If so, how? _____

_____

(Note other questions you asked below with the answers or any comments you have about the interview.)

_____

_____

_____

_____

_____

_____

_____

_____

_____

_____

Activity 4: Experience Traditional Music

Goal: To become familiar with a traditional or folk music style, its instruments, its performers, and its performance context.

Attend a folk music session of your choice, either in an informal performance setting, such as a coffee house or a folk festival, or in a concert hall, perhaps as a sponsored campus event.

Complete the questions below.

Date of event: _____ Location: _____

Title of event: _____

Performers or groups heard: _____

_____

Folk culture(s) represented: _____

_____

Which instruments were played? _____

_____

Describe the singing style (if applicable). _____

_____

Was there dancing? _____ If so, what style and dance types?

_____

_____

Were the performers in costume? _____ If so, describe the costumes.

_____

_____

Describe the performance setting and its atmosphere.

_____

_____

_____

_____

What are some of the musical characteristics of this traditional music style (consider melody, rhythm and meter, harmony, and texture)?

_____

_____

_____

_____

_____

Try to talk with the performers during a break (at an informal event) or after the concert. Musicians generally welcome questions about their performance or instruments. How did the musicians become interested in this particular traditional style?

_____

_____

_____

Is it part of their cultural heritage? _____

Ask about the instruments or dancing and describe their comments below.

_____

_____

_____

_____

What did you most enjoy about the event? _____

_____

Would you attend another concert like this one? _____

Activity 5: Experience an International Night Out

Goal: To hear live music from another culture, in either a concert or a restaurant setting.

Attend a concert on campus or in the community by a non-Western group (a solo performer or a choral, instrumental, or dance group), or go to an international restaurant that features live traditional music.

Complete the questions below.

Date of event: _____ Place: _____

Was this a _____ concert or _____ restaurant entertainment?

Names of performers: _____

_____

Country or culture of origin: _____

Did you hear singing? _____ yes _____ no

If so, describe the style you heard. _____

_____

Did you hear instruments? _____ yes _____ no

If so, which instruments? _____

_____

Did you see dancing? _____ yes _____ no

If so, what style of dancing was it? _____

_____

Were the performers in native costume? _____ yes _____ no

If so, describe them. _____

_____

Do you know the titles of any works performed? _____ yes _____ no

If so, list some. _____

_____

Describe in your own words the music you heard (consider the melody, rhythm, harmony, and texture).

_____

_____

_____

_____

_____

_____

_____

Did you like the music? _____ yes _____ no

Why or why not? _____

_____

If you attended a restaurant, did you eat ethnic food? _____ yes _____ no

If yes, what kinds? _____

_____

Did you like the food? _____ yes _____ no

Is this the first time you have heard live music of this style? _____ yes _____ no

Would you go to another concert/restaurant entertainment of the same type?

_____ yes _____ no

Activity 6: Explore PBS Programming

Goal: To become more aware of the diverse music programs and live performances available on PBS (the Public Broadcasting System).

Find a TV station in your area that is affiliated with PBS, and review the programming for a week. Watch any style of music program and discuss it below.

Program title: _____

Station: _____ Date/time of program: _____

Major performers/groups: _____

_____

_____

Titles of selected works (if known): _____

_____

_____

What type of music was performed?

___ classical. What eras? _____

___ popular. What styles? _____

___ traditional. What styles? _____

___ non-Western. What styles? _____

___ dramatic music. Was it a(n) ___ opera ___ ballet ___ musical ___ other?

List other music programs offered during the week. _____

_____

_____

_____

_____

_____

_____

Describe the performance in your own words. Mention some elements of musical style, and evaluate the performance.

_____

_____

_____

_____

_____

_____

_____

_____

_____

_____

_____

_____

_____

_____

_____

Did you enjoy the program? ___ yes ___ no ___ somewhat

Would you have enjoyed it ___ more ___ less ___the same if you had been at the live performance?

Comments: _____

_____

_____

_____

_____

Activity 7: View Opera from Home

Goal: To become familiar with an opera of your choice and its characteristic traits.

Go to your local video store or campus or public library, select an opera video that interests you, watch it, and describe it below.

Opera title: _____

Composer: _____

When was the opera written? _____

In what language is it sung? _____

Did the video have English subtitles? ____ yes ____ no

Which opera company performed? _____

Name the leading solo performers (check credits or box).

_____

_____

_____

Who are the main characters in the opera? _____

_____

_____

_____

Summarize the plot below. _____

_____

_____

_____

_____

_____

_____

_____

_____

_____

_____

_____

_____

_____

_____

_____

_____

_____

_____

_____

Was this ___ comic or ____ serious opera?

Did it begin with an instrumental overture? ____ yes ___ no

Check below the vocal styles that you heard.

___ aria   ___ recitative ___ solo ensemble   ___ chorus

Describe the music in your own words. _____

_____

_____

_____

_____

_____

Did you enjoy the opera? ___ yes ___ no ___ somewhat

Would you like to see another? ___ yes ___ no

If yes, ___ on video or ___ in live performance?

Comments: _____

_____

_____

_____

_____

Activity 8: Explore a Music Video Network

Goal: To assess the programming on a music video network and the impact the network has had on popular music.

Review MTV (or another music video network) programming for two or three days, choose several diverse music programs to watch, and answer the following questions.

Name of network selected: _____

Program (1) title: _____

Date: _____ Time: _____ Program length: _____

Program (2) title: _____

Date: _____ Time: _____ Program length: _____

List some of the other programs offered that you did not select.

_____

_____

_____

Describe program 1 (groups performing, focus, or theme).

_____

_____

_____

_____

_____

What styles of popular music were included?

___ soft rock	___ punk rock
___ folk rock	___ reggae
___ jazz rock	___ rap
___ art rock	___ grunge rock
___ Latin rock	___ new wave
___ heavy metal	

other _____

Describe one musical style you heard and its characteristics.

_____

_____

Describe program 2 (groups performing, focus, or theme).

_____

_____

_____

_____

_____

_____

What styles of popular music were included?

___ soft rock	___ punk rock
___ folk rock	___ reggae
___ jazz rock	___ rap
___ art rock	___ grunge rock
___ Latin rock	___ new wave
___ heavy metal	

other: _____

Describe one musical style you heard and its characteristics.

_____

_____

Do you watch MTV or another music video network often? ___ yes ___ no
___ sometimes

Do you prefer ___ watching a video network or ___ listening to a CD or mp3?

Explain your answer. _____

_____

What effect do you think MTV and other video networks have had on the popular music industry?

_____

_____

Activity 9: Relive the Woodstock Festival of 1969

Goal: To become familiar with various 1960s-era rock groups and styles through a historic event.

Go to your college or public library or to a video store to get a DVD of the original Woodstock Festival, held in 1969. Watch several of the following now-classic performances:

Performer/Group	Song
Richie Havens	*Freedom* (adapted from *Motherless Child*)
Joan Baez	*Joe Hill*
	Swing Low, Sweet Chariot
The Who	*We're Not Gonna Take It*
	Summertime Blues
Sha-Na-Na	*At the Hop*
Joe Cocker	*With a Little Help from My Friends*
Country Joe and the Fish	*Rock and Soul Music*
Arlo Guthrie	*Comin' into Los Angeles*
Crosby, Stills and Nash	*Judy Blue Eyes*
Ten Years After	*I'm Going Home*
John Sebastian	*Rainbows All over Your Blues*
Country Joe MacDonald	*I Feel Like I'm Fixin' to Die Rag*
Santana	*Soul Sacrifice*
Sly and the Family Stone	*I Want to Take You Higher*
Jimi Hendrix	*The Star-Spangled Banner*

Select three performances representing different groups and styles and answer the following questions.

Group (1): _____

Title (1): _____

What style of rock is this? _____

Did you know the group or song prior to this video?

___ group ___ song ___ both

Describe the musical elements of the style. _____

_____

_____

_____

Group (2): _____

Title (2): _____

What style of rock is this? _____

Did you know the group or song prior to this video?

___ group ___ song ___ both

Describe the musical elements of the style. _____

_____

_____

_____

Group (3): _____

Title (3): _____

What style of rock is this? _____

Did you know the group or song prior to this video?

___ group ___ song ___ both

Describe the musical elements of the style. _____

_____

_____

_____

Why is this Woodstock Festival remembered as a historic event? _____

_____

_____

_____

Activity 10: Sing Karaoke

Goal: To be actively involved in music performance as an amateur singer.

Find a karaoke club in your area, or check out or buy a karaoke track to use at home or in class, and perform as a solo singer or with a group. (If you are unsure what karaoke is, look it up in your text.)

Date: _____ Location: _____

List the song(s) you sang: _____

_____

_____

List songs others sang: _____

_____

_____

Did you know the words for the songs you sang? ___ yes ___ no

Did you have the words available to look at? ___ yes ___ no

If yes, did you have ___ a printed text or ___ a monitor?

Did you sing ___ as a soloist or ___ with a group?

Describe how it felt to be a singer. _____

_____

_____

_____

_____

_____

Were you able to sing in tune (on pitch)?

___ yes   ___ no ___ sometimes

Do you think you have a good singing voice? ___ yes ___ no

Did other singers sing in tune?

___ yes ___ no ___ sometimes

Describe how one of the other singers sounded. _____

_____

_____

Did others have good singing voices?

___ yes ___ no ___ some did

In your opinion, what determines a good voice? _____

_____

_____

_____

Where did the tradition of karaoke singing originate?

_____

What do you think accounts for its popularity? _____

_____

_____

Have you ever done this before? ___ yes ___ no

Would you enjoy trying it again? ___ yes ___ no

Activity 11: Engage in Group Singing

Goal: To study imitation through the singing of a round.

The song below is a famous round titled *Sumer is icumen in,* or the Sumer Canon. The song is in medieval English and dates from the thirteenth century. It has a melody that can be sung as a four-voice round, with two additional lower voices singing an ostinato (called a *pes,* pronounced "pace").

Practice singing the melody line together, then learn the two lower parts. To sing as a round, divide into melody singers (two, three, or four people or groups) and ostinato, or *pes,* singers (two people or groups). Have the two lower parts begin (they will help keep time), then have melody group 1 enter, then group 2, then 3, and finally 4, in overlapping imitation. Each group enters with the melody, starting when the previous group reaches number 2 in the music; each continues through the whole piece, repeating it as many times as needed. Remember that a round can go on indefinitely, so decide how many times you will sing the work before you begin.

Note that the lower parts are notated in the bass clef. (*Performance note:* The music is transposed to C major. A score of the resulting piece is on the next page. Instruments may be used instead of voices on any part.)

Poem	*Translation (modern English)*
Sing cuccu; sing cuccu, nu	Sing cuckoo; sing cuckoo, now
Sing cuccu, nu sing cuccu!	Sing cuckoo, now sing cuckoo!
Sumer is icumen in,	Summer is coming on,
Lhude sing cuccu!	Loudly sing cuckoo!
Groweth sed and bloweth med,	The seeds are growing and the
	meadow is blooming,
And springth the wde nu.	And the woods are budding.
Sing cuccu!	Sing cuckoo!
Awe bleteth after lomb,	The ewe bleats for the lamb,
Lhouth after calve cu;	The cow lows for the calf;
Bulloc sterteth,	The bullock jumps,
Bucke verteth,	The buck breaks wind,
Murie sing cuccu.	Merrily sing cuckoo.
Cuccu, cuccu,	Cuckoo, cuckoo,
Wel singes thu cuccu,	Well you sing cuckoo,
Ne swik thu naver nu.	Do not ever stop now.

241

Melody and 2 short *pes* (ostinato) parts:

Resulting music when sung as a round, showing imitation of lines:

Activity 12: Write a Rap Song

Goal: To understand what musical elements make up rap and to create within the style.

Create a rap song of your own composition. Since rap is a combination of rhymed lyrics spoken or recited over a rhythm track, you have two different tasks:

1. Create a rhythm track with a steady beat. You can do this in one of four ways:
   a. record simple rhythmic patterns you make up and play;
   b. record a "sample" from sounds or older prerecorded pieces;
   c. use a prerecorded rhythm setting on an electronic keyboard or drum machine; or
   d. buy a rap rhythm track in a music store.

If you write your own rhythmic accompaniment, it can be very simple. Think in terms of long (L) and short (S) durations, and make it in quadruple meter. Here is an example that should be counted in 4 at a quick pace (notice it begins with an upbeat):

SSL   SL SSL SL SSL SL
4 1 2 3 4 1 2 3 4 1 2 3

2. Write a text (typically rhymed) to recite over the accompaniment track. Your text should be about some current issue (political, social, or environmental).

Do you listen to rap? ___ yes ___ no ___ sometimes

Which groups do you know? _____

_____

_____

_____

What is the subject matter of the rap songs you know? _____

_____

_____

_____

_____

Describe how you created a rhythm track for your song.

_____

_____

_____

_____

_____

_____

Write your song text in the space below.

_____

_____

_____

_____

_____

_____

_____

_____

_____

_____

What do you like or dislike about rap from a musical point of view?

_____

_____

_____

_____

_____

Activity 13: Play in a Percussion Ensemble

Goal: To understand polyrhythm through the spontaneous creation of a group rhythmic work.

Work with a small group of three to six students, each providing a percussion instrument of his or her choice. This instrument can be anything that produces either a definite or an indefinite pitch. Ideally, the instruments should have differing timbres.

1. Choose a master percussionist, or leader, to give signals to play and stop.

2. Choose a number to determine the overall rhythmic cycle (the example below is based on 12). Have each player determine a different pattern to play within that cycle, as in additive meters. Be sure to keep a steady beat throughout.

```
Player 1   1 2 3 4 5 6 7 8 9 10 11 12
           X   X   X X   X   X      X

Player 2   1 2 3 4 5 6 7 8 9 10 11 12
           X X   X X   X X   X  X

Player 3   1 2 3 4 5 6 7 8 9 10 11 12
           X     X     X     X

Player 4   1 2 3 4 5 6 7 8 9 10 11 12
           X X X   X X X   X  X  X
```

3. Play the piece, allowing one instrument to start, then adding others. You may wish to have one player count out loud. As the sound builds to a climax, players may decide to improvise on their patterns. Watch the master percussionist for a cue to stop. Try this several times until you are satisfied with the result, then try other patterns.

List the percussion instruments used.

Player 1: _____

Player 2: _____

Player 3: _____

Player 4: _____

Player 5: _____

Player 6: _____

Which player was designated the master percussionist? _____

245

4. Make a musical score by aligning the different beat patterns chosen by the performers (the grid below allows for patterns of up to 19 beats).

Player
1 _|_|_|_|_|_|_|_|_|_|_|_|_|_|_|_|_|_|_|
2 _|_|_|_|_|_|_|_|_|_|_|_|_|_|_|_|_|_|_|
3 _|_|_|_|_|_|_|_|_|_|_|_|_|_|_|_|_|_|_|
4 _|_|_|_|_|_|_|_|_|_|_|_|_|_|_|_|_|_|_|
5 _|_|_|_|_|_|_|_|_|_|_|_|_|_|_|_|_|_|_|
6 _|_|_|_|_|_|_|_|_|_|_|_|_|_|_|_|_|_|_|
  1 2 3 4 5 6 7 8 9 10 11 12 13 14 15 16 17 18 19

Were players successful at keeping a steady beat?

___ yes ___ no ___ somewhat

What were the difficulties in the performance? _____

_____

_____

_____

Did players freely improvise during the performance?

___ yes ___ no ___ some did

Describe how you achieved polyrhythm in your composition.

_____

_____

_____

Evaluate your musical efforts. _____

_____

_____

_____

Activity 14: Sample a Music Group on the Web

Goal: To use the Web as a resource for information about a performing group, its activities, and its recordings.

Choose a current music performance group (rock, jazz, folk, or classical) that you do NOT know well and locate one or more Web sites with information on the group.

Group selected: _____

How many sites did you find? _____

Does the group have its own official site? _____

Are there many "fan" sites for the group? _____

Peruse one or more of the sites to answer the following questions.

Who are the performers in the group? _____

_____

What instruments, if any, do they play? _____

_____

What style of music does the group represent? _____

Is there historical information about the group? _____

If so, summarize its history here. _____

_____

Is there a discography provided? _____ Which recording company

issues the group's music? _____

Is there a current schedule posted for the group? _____

If so, where could you go to hear the group live? _____

Are there links provided to other related sites? _____

If so, what kind of sites are linked? _____

Is it possible to hear musical examples? _____

If so, follow the directions to hear a sample of the group's music. Which work did you select? _____

Describe the style of the work in your own words. _____

_____

_____

_____

Can you purchase recordings by the group on the same or a linked site? _____

Are you interested in hearing more music by this group? ___ yes ___ no

What do you like or dislike about the group's music? _____

_____

_____

_____

How do you think the Web has facilitated the spread of music by this group and other groups like it? _____

_____

_____

_____

_____

_____

Activity 15: Sample a Modern Composer on the Web

Goal: To use the Web to "meet" a modern composer, learn of the composer's recent artistic activities, and hear a sample of music by the composer.

Find the Web site of a living composer. Consider some of those discussed in your text, such as John Adams, Libby Larsen, Andrew Lloyd Webber, or Stephen Sondheim.

Which composer did you select? _____

What is the URL of their Web site? _____

Is the site posted by _____ the composer or _____ a commercial firm?

Are there other sites for this composer? _____

If so, how many? _____

What kind of information is posted on the site you selected?

_____

_____

In which genres does this composer write? _____

_____

What are the composer's recent projects? _____

_____

_____

What composition awards has this composer won? _____

_____

Is there a discography of available recordings listed? _____

Which recording company publishes this composer's works?

_____

Is it possible to hear music examples? _____

If so, follow the directions to hear something by the composer.

What did you select? _____

Describe the style in your own words. _____

_____

_____

_____

What general musical style would this selection be considered?

             ____ avant-garde   ____ jazz-inspired

             ____ minimalism   ____ rock-inspired

             ____ New Romanticism   ____ musical theater

             other _____

What did you like about the sample you heard of the composer's music?

_____

_____

Would you be interested in hearing more works by this composer?

___ yes   ___ perhaps, but in a different style   ___ no

CONCERT REPORTS

The following section is designed to guide you in knowing what to listen for at concerts and how to write a concert report. Prior to going to a concert, be sure to read pages 4–11 in your text, "Attending Concerts," to help you know what to expect, to learn traditional concert etiquette, and to assist you in finding interesting programs on your campus or in your community.

There are five concert report outlines in this section, each designed for a particular type of program. The questions vary slightly, depending on whether the works are vocal or instrumental, and whether the performance includes classical, popular, or world music. The forms ask that you focus your attention on one or two selections to describe in some detail. Some concerts offer a mixture of styles and genres; in these cases, use either report form 1 or 2, or ask your instructor for advice. The report forms provided are:

1. Instrumental music (for orchestras, bands, chamber music, and solo recitals)
2. Choral/Vocal music (for choirs, choruses, and solo vocalists)
3. Dramatic music (for operas, musicals, and plays with music)
4. Popular music (for rock and jazz groups or soloists)
5. World music (for traditional and non-Western groups or soloists)

This section begins with a sample outline and report, based on the program reproduced on the following page. These are meant to serve as guidelines in approaching your assignment or project. Your instructor may ask you to submit a written report only, in which case you may want to take the outline form with you to the concert and use it to jot down your own notes. Alternatively, your instructor may wish to have only the completed outline, or both the report form and a prose report. You will probably be asked to submit a copy of the concert program and perhaps to attach the canceled ticket stub. Be sure to find out what your instructor requires before completing any assignment.

PROGRAM

Overture to *A Midsummer Night's Dream*   Felix Mendelssohn
                                                            (1809–1847)

Symphony No. 41 in C major, K. 551   W. A. Mozart
  (*Jupiter*)   (1756–1791)
    Allegro vivace
    Andante cantabile
    Menuetto (Allegretto) & Trio
    Finale (Molto allegro)

INTERMISSION

Concerto No. 1 for Piano and Orchestra   P. I. Tchaikovsky
  in B-flat minor, Op. 23   (1840–1893)
    Allegro non troppo e molto maestoso; Allegro con spirito
    Andantino simplice; Prestissimo; Tempo I
    Allegro con fuoco

Barbara Allen, piano

The University Symphony Orchestra
Eugene Castillo, conductor

Sample Outline: Concert Report 1: Instrumental Music

(Orchestra)   ATTACH
Band   TICKET
Chamber music   STUB
Solo recital   HERE

Concert Setting

Date of concert: *September 22, 2007*

Place of concert: *Carpenter Performing Arts Center*

Name of group(s) performing: *University Symphony*
Orchestra, Eugene Castillo, conductor

Briefly describe the concert setting (hall, performers' dress).

the hall was large — over 1,000 seats

performers wore black (formal dress)

Were concert programs provided? ✓ yes ___ no. If yes, attach a copy.

Were program notes provided? ✓ yes ___ no

Were there any spoken remarks about the concert? ___ yes ✓ no

Could you follow the order of the concert? ✓ yes ___ no

Were there any aspects of concert conventions that surprised you? *yes*

Which? *latecomers were not admitted until after the first piece began*

Concert Music

Which genres of music were performed (such as symphony or sonata)?

overture, symphony, concerto

_____

Did you read about any of the works performed? ✓ yes ___ no

If yes, where? ✓ program notes ___ textbook ___ outside reading

Were any of the works programmatic (with literary or pictorial associations)?

✓ yes ___ no

If yes, which? *Overture to A Midsummer Night's Dream*

What historical eras were represented on the program?

___ pre-1600 ___ Baroque ✓ Classical ✓ Romantic ___ 20th century

Choose two works from the program. Name the composer, the work, and the movement (if applicable), and compare the works in the following outline.

	FIRST WORK	SECOND WORK
Composer:	*Mendelssohn*	*Tchaikovsky*
Title:	*A Midsummer Night's Dream*	*Concerto No. 1 for Piano*
Movement or Section:	*opening*	*First*
Melody:	*high range and disjunct, later conjunct*	*wide range—sweeping*
Rhythm/ Meter:	*duple*	*triple*
Harmony:	*consonant*	*a little dissonant*
Texture:	*homophonic*	*homophonic*
Tempo:	*Allegro (very fast)*	*Allegro (fast)*
Dynamics:	*soft at opening, then grows louder*	*loud (forte) for opening—later soft*
Instruments:	*woodwinds begin, then strings, later full orchestra*	*begins with French horns, then piano and full orchestra*
Mood:	*enchanted*	*dramatic*
Other:		

What was your overall reaction to the concert?

    ✓ enjoyed it a lot   ____ enjoyed it somewhat

    ____ did not enjoy it much   ____ did not enjoy it at all

What did you like about it? *the orchestra was all students*

What did you not like about it? *noisy students in the audience*

Other comments: ____

I attended the University Symphony Orchestra concert on Saturday night, September 22. The group was made up of student musicians and was conducted by Eugene Castillo. The pianist, Barbara Allen, is a music faculty member.

The concert hall was larger than I expected—it seated over 1,000 people, and it was nearly full. I had a good seat about halfway back in the hall. The orchestra was already on stage when I arrived. When the lights went down, the first violinist stood up and signaled the oboe player to play a note to tune the orchestra. Next, the conductor entered and led the orchestra in the first work, the Overture to *A Midsummer Night's Dream* by Mendelssohn, an early Romantic composer. The notes on my program explained that this was a programmatic work based on the Shakespeare play, which I had read in high school. It was easy to follow the melodies for the different characters. The first theme was played by the strings in a high range, very lightly, reminding me of the fairies in the play. Later, the strings played a smooth, conjunct melody that was the love theme. This was followed by a humorous, disjunct theme, reminding me of the braying donkey in the play. All these themes returned near the end of the piece. The work was in duple meter and was mostly consonant.

The next work was a symphony by Mozart, his last, according to the program. It had four movements and was written in a major key. The first movement was an Allegro in sonata-allegro form. Then came a slow movement, followed by a triple-meter minuet. The last movement was the fastest of all, with a mostly conjunct opening melody. This work was written in the Classical era.

After the intermission, the orchestra and the soloist, Barbara Allen, played a piano concerto by the late Romantic Russian composer Tchaikovsky. This piece was long and very dramatic. The first movement had several sections. It began fast, first with the French horns, then the piano entered with disjunct chords. The strings introduced the first melody. The piano soloist played without music, and her part seemed very difficult. Her hands moved quickly as she played high and low notes on the piano. This piece was more dissonant than the other works on the program. The second movement was quiet and melancholy in mood, with a fast middle section. The last movement was in triple meter and sounded like a dance.

I enjoyed this concert very much, except for some noisy students sitting in front of me. I was impressed with how well the student musicians could play. I hope to be able to attend more concerts on campus in the future.

Concert Report 1: Instrumental Music

Orchestra   ATTACH
Band   TICKET
Chamber music   STUB
Solo recital   HERE

Concert Setting

Date of concert: _____

Place of concert: _____

Name of group(s) performing: _____

_____

Briefly describe the concert setting (hall, performers' dress):

_____

_____

Were concert programs provided? ___ yes ___ no. If yes, attach a copy.

Were program notes provided? ___ yes ___ no

Were there any spoken remarks about the concert? ___ yes ___ no

Could you follow the order of the concert? ___ yes ___ no

Were there any aspects of concert conventions that surprised you? _____

Which? _____

Concert Music

Which genres of music were performed (such as symphony or sonata)?

_____

_____

Did you read about any of the works performed? ___ yes ___no

If yes, where? ___ program notes ___ textbook ___ outside reading

Were any of the works programmatic (with literary or pictorial

associations)? ___ yes ___ no

If yes, which? _____

What historical eras were represented on the program?

___ pre-1600 ___ Baroque ___ Classical ___ Romantic ___ 20th century

257

Choose two works from the program. Name the composer, the work, and the movement (if applicable) and compare the works in the following outline:

	FIRST WORK	SECOND WORK
Composer:	_____	_____
Title:	_____	_____
Movement or Section:	_____	_____
Melody:	_____	_____
	_____	_____
Rhythm/ Meter:	_____	_____
Harmony:	_____	_____
	_____	_____
Texture:	_____	_____
	_____	_____
Tempo:	_____	_____
	_____	_____
Dynamics:	_____	_____
	_____	_____
Instruments:	_____	_____
	_____	_____
Mood:	_____	_____
Other:	_____	_____

What was your overall reaction to the concert?
    ___ enjoyed it a lot   ___ enjoyed it somewhat
    ___ did not enjoy it much   ___ did not enjoy it at all

What did you like about it? _____

_____

What did you not like about it? _____

_____

Other comments: _____

_____

_____

Concert Report 2: Choral/Vocal Music

Choir/Chorus   ATTACH
Chamber choir/Madrigal choir   TICKET
Solo vocal recital   STUB
                                         HERE

Concert Setting

Date of concert: _____

Place of concert: _____

Name of group(s) performing: _____

_____

Describe briefly the group(s) performing (size, men vs. women):

_____

_____

Were concert programs provided? ___ yes ___ no. If yes, attach a copy.

Were program notes provided? ___ yes ___ no

Did the program include:

     the vocal texts that were sung? ___ yes ___ no

     translations of foreign language texts? ___ yes ___ no

Did the concert include instrumental accompaniment? ___ yes ___ no

If yes, check those applicable ____ orchestra ____ small instrumental group

____ harpsichord ____ piano ____ organ ____ other (specify)_____

Concert Music

Did the program include any of the following genres?

Choral		Solo vocal
___ Mass	___ oratorio	___ opera aria
___ part song	___ madrigal	___ Lieder
___ anthem	___ hymn	___ song cycle
___ motet	___ cantata	

List any other genres performed. _____

_____

Did you read about any of the works performed? ___ yes ___ no

If yes, where? ___ program notes ___ textbook ___ outside reading

259

What historical eras were represented on the program?

___ Medieval/Renaissance   ___ Baroque   ___ Classical

___Romantic   ___ 20th century

Choose two works from the program. Name the composer, the work, and the movement (if applicable) and compare them in the following outline.

	FIRST WORK	SECOND WORK
Composer:	_____	_____
Title:	_____	_____
Movement or Section:	_____	_____
Melody:	_____	_____
Rhythm/ Meter:	_____	_____
Harmony:	_____	_____
Texture:	_____	_____
Tempo:	_____	_____
Dynamics:	_____	_____
Vocal style:	_____	_____
Mood:	_____	_____
Other:	_____	_____

What was your overall reaction to the concert?

___ enjoyed it a lot   ____ enjoyed it somewhat

___ did not enjoy it much   ____ did not enjoy it at all

What did you like about it? _____

_____

What did you not like about it? _____

_____

Other comments: _____

_____

NAME   DATE   CLASS
_____   _____   _____

Concert Report 3: Dramatic Music

Opera/Operetta   ATTACH
Musical   TICKET
Play with incidental music   STUB
                                                  HERE

Concert Setting

Date of concert: _____ Location: _____

Composer/Author: _____

Title of work: _____

Were concert programs provided? ___ yes ___ no. If yes, attach a copy.

Were program notes provided? ___ yes ___ no

Did the program include:

    the vocal texts that were sung? ___ yes ___ no

    translations of foreign language texts? ___ yes ___ no

    a summary of the plot or action? ___ yes ___ no

Concert Music

In what language was the work performed? _____

In what language was it originally written? _____

Did you read about the work performed? ___ yes ___ no

If yes, where? ___ program notes ___ textbook ___ outside reading

Give a brief summary of the plot of this work.

_____

_____

_____

_____

Did the performance include instrumental accompaniment? ___ yes ___ no

If yes, was the music: ___ live or ___ prerecorded?

What instruments were employed? If live, where were they placed?

_____

_____

Choose a selection from the work (an aria, a song, or an instrumental number), identify it in some way, and describe its musical features below.

Composer: _____

Selection: _____

Melody: _____

_____

Rhythm/meter: _____

_____

Harmony: _____

_____

Texture: _____

_____

Tempo: _____

_____

Dynamics: _____

_____

Vocal style: _____

_____

Instrumental style: _____

_____

Mood: _____

Other: _____

What was your overall reaction to the concert?
___ enjoyed it a lot   ___ enjoyed it somewhat
___ did not enjoy it much   ___ did not enjoy it at all

What did you like about it? _____

_____

What did you not like about it? _____

_____

Other comments: _____

_____

_____

Concert Report 4: Popular Music

Rock group   ATTACH
Solo singer or Instrumentalist   TICKET
Jazz combo or Ensemble   STUB
                                                                HERE

Concert Setting

Date of concert: _____

Place of concert: _____

Name of group(s): _____

_____

Did you know about the performer or group prior to this concert?
    ___ from recordings   ___ from MTV or radio
    ___ from a friend   ___ did not know

Concert Music

What was the makeup (instruments and voices) of the performance?

_____

_____

_____

How would you describe the style or genre of music performed?

_____

_____

Choose a selection from the concert and describe it below.

Selection: _____

Melody: _____

_____

Rhythm/meter: _____

_____

Harmony: _____

_____

Texture: _____

_____

Tempo: _____

_____

Dynamics: _____

_____

Vocal style: _____

_____

Instrumental style: _____

_____

Mood: _____

Other: _____

What was your overall reaction to the concert?

___ enjoyed it a lot   ____ enjoyed it somewhat
___ did not enjoy it much   ____ did not enjoy it at all

What did you like about it? _____

_____

What did you not like about it? _____

_____

Other comments: _____

_____

_____

Concert Report 5: World Music

ATTACH
TICKET
STUB
HERE

Concert Setting

Date of concert: _____

Place of concert: _____

Name of group(s): _____

_____

Country(ies) or culture(s) represented in concert: _____

_____

Was there a concert program? ___ yes ___ no

Were there any: program notes? ___ yes ___ no

               spoken remarks? ___ yes ___ no

Concert Music

What was the makeup (instruments and voices) of the performance?

_____

_____

_____

_____

What was unfamiliar to you about the music and its performance?

_____

_____

_____

What was familiar to you about it? _____

_____

_____

_____

Choose a selection from the concert and describe it below.

Selection: _____

Melody: _____

_____

Rhythm/meter: _____

_____

Harmony: _____

_____

Texture: _____

_____

Tempo: _____

_____

Dynamics: _____

_____

Vocal style: _____

_____

Instrumental style: _____

_____

Mood: _____

Other: _____

What was your overall reaction to the concert?
___ enjoyed it a lot   ____ enjoyed it somewhat
___ did not enjoy it much   ____ did not enjoy it at all

What did you like about it? _____

_____

What did you not like about it? _____

_____

Other comments: _____

_____

_____

266

Post-Course Survey

Level:

___ Freshman ___ Sophomore ___ Junior ___ Senior ___ Graduate

___ High School ___ Adult Education ___ Other _____

Major (or undeclared): _____

Minor (or undeclared): _____

Have your musical preferences:

___ changed, ___ expanded, or ___ remained the same?

Which genres did you most enjoy studying in this course?

___ orchestral music ___ chamber music ___ opera ___ musical

___ choral music ___ ballet ___ solo vocal music ___ rock

___ jazz ___ traditional music ___ world music

Rate your general reaction to the music of the various style periods:

   a. like very much   c. do not like very much
   b. like somewhat   d. dislike

___ Middle Ages   ___ Renaissance   ___ Baroque

___ Classical   ___ Romantic   ___ 20th century

List two specific pieces that you enjoyed very much.

_____

_____

What about them appealed to you? _____

_____

List two pieces that you did not enjoy hearing.

_____

_____

What about them did not appeal to you? _____

_____

Musical Listening

During this course, did you:

___ attend concerts?   If so, how many? _____

___ watch TV broadcasts of concerts?   If so, how many? _____

___ watch videos of concerts?   If so, how many? _____

Do you enjoy attending concerts? ___ yes   ___ no

Will you now try new types of concerts? ___ yes   ___ no   ___ maybe

Have you purchased any musical materials during the course (other than

required materials)? ___ yes ___ no

If yes, what have you purchased? _____

_____

_____

Course Assessment

What was most valuable about the course content? _____

_____

_____

What was most valuable about the textbook? _____

_____

_____

Was this study guide helpful to you in the course?   ___ yes ___ no

Would you like to take another music course?   ___ yes ___ no

If yes, what focus would you most enjoy?

    ___ classical music   ___ world music   ___ jazz   ___ rock

    ___ music theory ___ performance ___ other _____

Other comments: _____

_____

_____